go deeper retreats

12 life-changing weekends for youth ministry

Group

Loveland, Colorado

Group's R.E.A.L. Guarantee to you:

Every Group resource incorporates our R.E.A.L. approach to ministry—a unique philosophy that results in long-term retention and life transformation. It's ministry that's:

**This is EARL.
He's R.E.A.L.
mixed up.
(Get it?)**

Relational
Because student-to-student interaction enhances learning and builds Christian friendships.

Experiential
Because what students experience sticks with them up to 9 times longer than what they simply hear or read.

Applicable
Because the aim of Christian education is to be both hearers and doers of the Word.

Learner-based
Because students learn more and retain it longer when the process is designed according to how they learn best.

go deeper retreats: 12 life-changing weekends for youth ministry
Copyright © 2002 Group Publishing, Inc.

Visit our Web site: **www.grouppublishing.com**

Credits
Contributing Authors: Jenny Baker, Steven L. Case, Paul E. Gauche, Mikal Keefer, Julia L. Roller, Christina Schofield, Alison Simpson, and Helen Turnbull
Editor: Kelli B. Trujillo
Creative Development Editor: Amy Simpson
Chief Creative Officer: Joani Schultz
Copy Editor: Linda Marcinkowski
Art Director: Kari K. Monson
Cover Art Director: Jeff A. Storm
Cover Designer: Alan Furst, Inc.
Computer Graphic Artist: Joyce Douglas
Illustrator: Amy Bryant
Production Manager: Dodie Tipton

Unless otherwise noted, Scripture taken from the HOLY BIBLE, NEW INTERNATIONAL VERSION®. Copyright © 1973, 1978, 1984 by International Bible Society. Used by permission of Zondervan Publishing House. All rights reserved.

ISBN 0-7644-2358-4
Printed in the United States of America.

contents

introduction

life-changing weekends

Deep faith…spiritual growth…life-change. These are the things you desire for your students—this is what you're working toward.

And these retreats will help you get there.

Retreats impact lives because they're opportunities to get students away from all of the competing influences in their lives and to help them focus on God, fellowship, and personal growth. They're a chance to help students stop and take a breather—to reflect on where they've been and to consider where they'd like to go. They're times to laugh, to cry, to experience true fellowship.

Go Deeper Retreats contains twelve complete retreat plans focused on topics that will help your students grow in their relationships with Jesus. In each retreat they'll key in on one specific Bible story and will explore it during the entire weekend, coming to understand the Scriptures in a deeper and more meaningful way. They'll dig into topics that are important to them, like friendship, serving others, dealing with doubt, or setting priorities. They'll develop intimate friendships with one another as they grow closer in small groups.

These life-changing weekends will help your students go deeper—in friendship, in fellowship, in faith.

how to use these retreats

Motto, Theme Verse, and Theme Song

Each retreat has a motto and a theme verse that summarize the main point of the weekend event. You may want to begin each teaching session by reviewing the theme and verse—or you could encourage students to memorize the motto and verse over the course of the retreat or lock-in. You can also use the motto and verse in pre-event publicity, on posters decorating your retreat site, or in follow-up postcards for your students.

Supplement the worship experiences on your retreat or lock-in by using songs from the CD *I Could Sing of Your Love Forever*. Each retreat has a Worship Idea tip, suggesting a song from the CD that ties in to the theme of the event. The two-CD set, songbook, and lyrics books are all available through Group Publishing (1-800-447-1070 or www.grouppublishing.com).

Master Supply List

Check out the Master Supply List at the beginning of each retreat to help you gather all of the supplies you'll need for each teaching session, small-group discussion, and student quiet time suggested in the retreat. (Note: This supply list does *not* include retreat basics such as sleeping bags, flashlights, or food—it only addresses the specifics for the various activities involved in the weekend.)

Suggested Schedules

Planning a Friday night through Sunday morning weekend retreat? Or a shorter, one-night lock-in? Toward the beginning of each retreat plan, you'll find two suggested schedules: one for a two-night retreat and one for a one-night retreat or lock-in. These schedules include the approximate time needed for each activity and teaching session; a listing of the specific supplies needed for each session; as well as suggestions for mealtimes, games, snacks, group activities, and free time.

Teaching Sessions

You won't find kids snoring on *these* retreats. The teaching sessions in this book are *far* from dull lectures or mini-sermons—they're active and interactive! Here's where students will really wrestle with the issues and will be challenged to apply God's truth to their lives. In addition to discussion and Bible study, during the four teaching sessions in each retreat you'll use the following methods to help your students dig deep into the Bible and apply Scripture to their lives.

Creative Projects—Get your teenagers' creative juices flowing with these hands-on projects that involve drawing, sculpting, painting, gluing, and designing. Look for the Creative Project icon in the margin of the teaching sessions.

Drama—Students will have the opportunity to test out their acting abilities in these interactive drama activities. Be on the lookout for the Drama icon and prepare to set the stage for fun!

Activities—Team challenge activities, games, and hands-on service projects are just some of the activities you'll find in the teaching sessions. Look for the Activity icon and get ready to move!

Creative Worship Experiences—Using symbolism, activities, objects, and unique prayer exercises, these experiences will take your students' perspectives on worship to a new level. Prepare yourself for a memorable experience when you see the Creative Worship Experience icon.

Movie Clips—Video clip illustrations and discussion-starters will grab your students' attention. Watch for the Movie Clip icon to know when to fire up the TV and VCR.

When using these G, PG, or PG-13 rated video clips, simply rewind your video (or DVD) to the moment when the studio logo for the movie appears, and set your timer at 0:00:00. Next, fast-forward to the suggested times. Make sure you preview these clips to be certain you have them cued up to the right spot! If your church is interested in using movie clips like these, you may obtain an umbrella license from the Motion Picture Licensing Corporation. Just visit www.mplc.com or call 1-800-462-8855 for more information.

Small Groups

Using small-group discussion is a powerful way to help students debrief what they've learned throughout the retreat. Each of these *Go Deeper* retreats includes small-group discussion questions to be used at the end of each day to help students process their experiences before they head to bed.

Each small group should consist of four to six students and one adult volunteer and should ideally be all guys or all girls. If your youth ministry already has a small-group or cell group program, go ahead and use these same groups for the retreat small-group discussion times. Otherwise, assign students to small groups at the beginning of the retreat. Be strategic by grouping students together with other students they may not know as well.

Adult leaders should be in charge of leading the small-group discussion sessions. Encourage adult leaders to really get to know their retreat small-group members and to listen attentively during the small-group discussion sessions.

Student Quiet Times

Every *Go Deeper* retreat includes opportunities for students to spend daily time alone with God. Using the "Student Quiet Time" handouts, students will do a variety of things—journal, read Scripture, pray, draw, or have a personal creative worship experience. Make sure the "Student Quiet Time" portion of the retreat is kept sacred—students should spread out and be alone, being careful not to distract each other.

Free Time, Group Activities, and Games

A retreat just isn't a retreat if it doesn't have free time, group activities, and games! You'll notice that each retreat schedule suggests a good chunk of time for these community-building activities. This downtime is really essential to give the students a chance to laugh together, catch up on rest, and build long-lasting memories.

Use some of your youth group's favorite games and team-building activities, or check out some of these great game books available from Group Publishing: *Jumpstarters: 100 Games to Spark Discussions; All-Star Games From All-Star Youth Leaders; The Gigantic Book of Games for Youth Ministry, Volume 1;* or *The Gigantic Book of Games for Youth Ministry, Volume 2.*

Leader Tips

Look in the margins to find lots of useful Leader Tips that will help you in facilitating various activities and discussions. In addition to these basic pointers, you'll also find tips that include customization ideas.

For Younger Teenagers—Some of the activities or discussions in the book may be too difficult for middle school or junior high students. These tips include ideas that will help you modify activities to meet young teenagers right where they're at.

For Extra Impact—Wanna go the extra mile? Pump up the experience to the extreme? Use the occasional For Extra Impact ideas in this book for higher prep projects that will make the experiences even more exciting.

getting ready to go!

Preparation

Preparing for these *Go Deeper Retreats* requires three important steps: planning, prayer, and personal study.

Planning—After you set a date and select a retreat location, determine cost and begin promotion!

❏ Recruit adult volunteers who will go on the retreat as chaperones and small-group leaders.

❏ Recruit adult volunteers to be in charge of planning and preparing meals.

❏ Coordinate transportation.

❏ Create a list of rules that all students need to follow on the retreat (such as conduct and safety rules).

❏ Secure parental permission for each student who will attend your retreat.

❏ Have parents fill out medical and liability release forms. (For more information on this, see pp. 225-229 of *Better Safe Than Sued* from Group Publishing.)

❏ Make sure parents have contact information for the retreat center.

❏ Give students copies of the "Stuff to Bring" list (p. 9).

❏ Pack a "Forget-Me-Not" box full of items that students may have forgotten, such as sunscreen, bug repellant, toothbrushes, and deodorant.

Prayer—Pray for each of the students who are attending the retreat. Enlist a team of parents or other adults who will commit to pray for the entire group during the event. Pray that God would prepare your own heart for the event—that you too will be stretched and challenged as you present the teaching session content.

Personal Study—A few weeks before the event, set aside some time each day for your own personal study of the retreat's Scripture focus. Take time to explore it, using study tools such as a concordance or a Bible dictionary. Journal your own thoughts and questions. Consider how the passage applies to your own life. Begin thinking of ways you can share your personal thoughts on the passage with your students during the retreat. Ask God to help you as you prepare to take your students deeper into God's Word.

STUFF TO BRING

Make sure you bring all of the items on this checklist to the retreat!

- ☐ BIBLE
- ☐ SLEEPING BAG
- ☐ PILLOW
- ☐ CLOTHING
- ☐ PAJAMAS
- ☐ NOTEBOOK
- ☐ PEN OR PENCIL
- ☐ TOOTHBRUSH AND TOOTHPASTE
- ☐ DEODORANT
- ☐ SHAMPOO AND CONDITIONER
- ☐ HAIRBRUSH
- ☐ HAIR DRYER AND CURLING IRON
- ☐ TOWELS
- ☐ FLASHLIGHT
- ☐ INSECT REPELLANT
- ☐ SUNSCREEN
- ☐
- ☐
- ☐
- ☐
- ☐

changed by grace

master supply list

In addition to basic retreat supplies such as food, games, Bibles, pens, pencils, paper, and worship music, you'll also need the following supplies:

❑ I newspaper for every four students
❑ glue sticks
❑ several pairs of scissors
❑ 2 sheets of poster board
❑ I photocopy of "Small-Group Discussion I" box (p. 13) for each small group
❑ *Cast Away* video (or DVD)
❑ VCR (or DVD player)
❑ TV
❑ 2 bottles of water
❑ flip chart
❑ marker
❑ I photocopy of "Student Quiet Time I: God's Grace Made Perfect in Weakness" (p. 17) for each student
❑ I water-soluble marker for each student
❑ paper or plastic cups
❑ *Aladdin* video (or DVD)
❑ handheld mirror
❑ I photocopy of "Small-Group Discussion 2" box (p. 16) for each small group
❑ I permanent marker for each student
❑ I photocopy of "Student Quiet Time 2: Marked by Grace" (p. 18) for each student
❑ optional: I white handkerchief for each student

retreat focus: Students will explore God's amazing grace by studying the story of Jesus' encounter with the woman at the well.

retreat motto: Face grace.

theme verse: "But he gives us more grace. That is why Scripture says: 'God opposes the proud but gives grace to the humble.' Submit yourselves, then, to God. Resist the devil, and he will flee from you" (James 4:6-7).

preparation

Before the retreat, gather all of the necessary supplies and make all of the photocopies recommended in the Master Supply List.

For Teaching Session 2, cue up *Cast Away* by setting the VCR counter at 0:00:00 when the studio logo appears before the movie starts. The segment you'll show starts at approximately 0:39:30 when Chuck begins sorting his packages. You'll also need to prepare one of your bottles of water by dropping some dirt or dust inside and swirling it around until the water is mucky and looks undrinkable.

For Teaching Session 3, make sure to cue up *Aladdin* by setting the VCR counter at 0:00:00 again when the studio logo appears and fast-forwarding to 0:54:00 when the genie says to the carpet, "So move!"

Make sure students are divided into small groups (for more information on this, see p. 7), and take some time to study John 4 on your own.

leader tip

Avoid the embarrassment of showing the wrong scene—preview movie clips before using them!

worship idea

For your theme song for the weekend, use "Better Is One Day" from the two-CD set *I Could Sing of Your Love Forever*. For information on ordering student lyrics books, a song leader book, and the CDs, call Group at 1-800-447-1070.

suggested schedule

2-Night Retreat

Day	Time	Activity	Supplies
Friday	6:00-7:00 p.m.	Games	
	7:00-8:00 p.m.	Teaching Session 1: Grace for All	Bibles, newspapers, scissors, glue sticks, poster board
	8:00-9:30 p.m.	Free Time or Games	
	9:30-10:00 p.m.	Small-Group Discussion 1	Photocopies of "Small-Group Discussion 1" box (p. 13)
	10:00-10:30 p.m.	Snacks	
	11:00 p.m.	Lights Out	
Saturday	8:00-9:00 a.m.	Breakfast	
	9:00-10:00 a.m.	Teaching Session 2: What Is Living Water?	Bibles, TV, VCR, *Cast Away* video, two bottles of water, flip chart and marker
	10:00-10:30 a.m.	Student Quiet Time 1: God's Grace Made Perfect in Weakness	Bibles, photocopies of "Student Quiet Time 1: God's Grace Made Perfect in Weakness" (p. 17), water-soluble markers, cups of water
	10:30 a.m.-noon	Free Time	
	noon-1:00 p.m.	Lunch	
	1:00-2:00 p.m.	Games	
	2:00-3:00 p.m.	Teaching Session 3: The Price of Grace	Bibles, TV, VCR, *Aladdin* video, mirror, cups of water
	3:00-5:00 p.m.	Free Time	
	5:00-6:00 p.m.	Dinner	
	6:00-9:30 p.m.	Games or Group Activities	
	9:30-10:00 p.m.	Small-Group Discussion 2	Photocopies of "Small-Group Discussion 2" box (p. 16)
	10:00-10:30 p.m.	Snacks	
	11:00 p.m.	Lights Out	
Sunday	7:30-8:00 a.m.	Student Quiet Time 2: Marked by Grace	Bibles, permanent markers, photocopies of "Student Quiet Time 2: Marked by Grace" (p. 18), pencils or pens Optional: white handkerchiefs
	8:00-9:00 a.m.	Breakfast	
	9:00-10:00 a.m.	Teaching Session 4: Living a Grace-Filled Life	Bibles, poster board and marker
	10:00 a.m.-noon	Games or Group Activities	

Day	Time	Activity	Supplies
Friday	6:00-7:00 p.m.	Games	
	7:00-8:00 p.m.	Teaching Session 1: Grace For All	Bibles, newspapers, scissors, glue sticks, poster board
	8:00-8:30 p.m.	Small-Group Discussion 1	Photocopies of "Small-Group Discussion 1" box (p. 13)
	8:30-9:00 p.m.	Free Time	
	9:00-10:00 p.m.	Teaching Session 3: The Price of Grace	Bibles, *Aladdin* video, TV, VCR, mirror, cups of water
	10:00-10:30 p.m.	Snacks	
	11:00 p.m.	Lights Out	
Saturday	7:30-8:00 a.m.	Student Quiet Time 1: God's Grace Made Perfect in Weakness	Bibles, photocopies of "Student Quiet Time 1: God's Grace Made Perfect in Weakness" (p. 17), water-soluble markers, cups of water
	8:00-9:00 a.m.	Breakfast	
	9:00-10:30 a.m.	Games or Group Activities	
	10:30-11:30 a.m.	Teaching Session 4: Living a Grace-Filled Life	Bibles, poster board, marker
	11:30 a.m.-noon	Student Quiet Time 2: Marked by Grace	Bibles, photocopies of "Student Quiet Time 2: Marked by Grace" (p. 18), permanent markers, pencils or pens Optional: white handkerchiefs

leader tip

You may want to begin each teaching session with five to ten minutes of singing. In addition to the suggested theme song, select other praise and worship songs that will complement the theme of the weekend.

teaching session 1: grace for all

Ask your students to form pairs and read John 4:1-9; Ephesians 2:1-10; and Romans 3:10 aloud to each other, trading off at the end of each verse. When everyone has finished, ask: • **How would you define *grace*?**

Say: **One way to define grace is "the unmerited love and favor of God toward mankind." Grace is a free gift. That's what is so amazing about it. We didn't do anything to deserve this present. We didn't offer any payment to God in the form of love or good deeds or extra-good prayers. Grace is God's response to our sins.**

Explain to the students that God's grace is meant for everyone. Challenge students to think about some limits they might set on grace, perhaps thinking that God's grace is limited to them, their friends, and their family. Prompt students to consider the message of Romans 3:10—that no one is righteous, and therefore no one has the right to put limits on grace.

Say: **Let's look at the example of the Samaritans. Does everybody remember the parable of the good Samaritan? Somebody summarize it for us.**

Wait for volunteers. If no one raises a hand, summarize the parable (found in Luke 10:30-37). Then explain that the story of the good Samaritan is striking because nobody thought a Samaritan could do something that good, that kind, that unselfish. Share with students a bit about the relationship between the Jews and the Samaritans, explaining that the Jews despised the Samaritans. Since they didn't follow the law, they were considered unclean, and so it was unthinkable for Jesus to even talk to a Samaritan, let alone a Samaritan woman.

Say: **Not only did Jesus single out a sinful Samaritan woman for a conversation, but he also chose to share with her one of his clearest messages about the power of God's grace. Jesus wanted us to know that grace is for everyone, not just those who followed the law or those who were socially acceptable.**

Have teenagers form groups of four, and pass out a newspaper to each group. Ask them to look through the articles and pick out a few that feature people who might be present-day Samaritans—people who are disliked by the rest of society. Some examples might include neo-Nazi skinheads, those convicted of crimes, or cruel political figures. Have them cut out the articles and paste them together onto a piece of poster board in the center of the room, creating one big collage.

Ask each group to share about who they picked and why.

Ask: • **Does God's grace apply to these people? Explain.**

• **Has this changed your ideas about grace? If so, how?**

Once students have finished sharing, lead them in a prayer, asking God to help them understand his limitless grace.

small-group discussion 1

Discuss these questions in your small group:

• The Samaritans were considered outcasts by the members of the Jewish community. Who are the Samaritans in your school? in your town? in your country?

• What do Jesus' actions teach us about judging others?

• How would you feel if somebody killed one of your family members and then accepted Jesus? Could you believe that God's grace was for that person, too?

teaching session 2: what is living water?

Ask a student to read John 4:10-14 aloud, then say: **Jesus uses living water as a metaphor for God's grace. Why did he choose water? Let's take a closer look at what water means to us.**

Show the movie clip from *Cast Away* starting at 0:39:30 when Chuck begins sorting packages. Stop at approximately 0:42:20 after he finally is able to drink some liquid from the coconut.

Ask: • **How did Chuck look when he was trying to get liquid from the coconut?**

• **Have you ever felt or looked as desperate as that? If so, what were the circumstances?**

Ask your teenagers to divide into groups of three, and have them come up with lists of all the ways they use water. Give them three to five minutes to do so, and then ask them to come back to the larger group and share their lists. Write all the uses of water on the flip chart.

Say: **Look at how important water is to us. Yet the living water of God puts all other water to shame. To compare living water to our drinking water is like comparing bottled water to a mud puddle.**

Pull out fresh bottled water and an identical bottle filled with muddied water. Say: **Look at the difference between these bottles. Would you drink out of this one?**

Offer the muddy bottle to one of your students, then pass both bottles around for students to look at.

Say: **I wouldn't want it, either. Compared to the living water of God's grace, the water our bodies need physically is like this muck. God's living water is more important than any of our other daily necessities—food, water, or shelter. Drinking water feeds our bodies; the living water feeds our eternal souls. When the Samaritan woman realized the extent of Jesus' promise of grace, she left her water jug at the well. In the face of God's grace, she realized that the water she needed to keep her body going was completely insignificant. She realized that one day in God's courts and in his grace is better than thousands elsewhere.**

leader tip

Need game ideas? Check out the game book suggestions on page 7!

teaching session 3: the price of grace

Set up a small side room for the activity at the end of this teaching session. Mount a mirror on the wall or place a handheld mirror on the table. On another table, place cups filled with water. Make sure there are enough cups of water for each student to have one.

Have students form pairs. Ask each pair to read John 4:15-26, switching readers every verse. When everyone has finished, ask: • **What would your natural reaction be if a stranger came to you and started to tell you what you were doing wrong with your life?**

Say: **Let's watch how a movie character reacts when his friend confronts him about his wrong behavior.**

Play the *Aladdin* clip starting at approximately 0:54:00 when the genie says, "So move!" Stop at approximately 0:56:40 when Princess Jasmine says, "Go jump off a balcony!"

Ask: • **In your opinion, how should Aladdin have handled the situation?**

• **How does Aladdin's reaction compare to the reaction of the Samaritan woman?**

• **Why did she react differently?**

Share with the students that one of the main differences between Aladdin's and the

Samaritan woman's reactions is that the Samaritan woman faced up to the sins in her life. She didn't deny what Jesus said, nor did she get angry. She accepted his words and the grace he offered her.

Say: **Experiencing God's grace requires our full cooperation. Accepting grace requires looking honestly at ourselves and working to bring our lives into line with God's will. There are two requirements for forgiveness and grace. The first is to repent.**

Ask: • **How would you define the word** *repent*?

Have a volunteer read Luke 13:3 aloud, then ask for students to think about and share examples of repentance, either from their own lives or in the lives of others they know.

Next invite a student to read John 1:12 aloud, and say: **The second requirement is to receive God's grace.**

Ask: • **In your opinion, what does the word** *receive* **mean in this verse?**

• **Did the Samaritan woman receive Jesus' grace? Defend your answer.**

Challenge your students to think of some examples from their own lives or others' lives of what it is like to receive grace. Ask for several students to share their examples.

Ask: • **Which is harder, repenting or receiving grace? Why?**

Say: **Once we have admitted our sins, it can be really hard to believe that we can be forgiven for them. But God's grace is so amazing, so abundant, that it** *does* **cover all of our sins. All we have to do is believe in grace and open ourselves to accept it.**

Instruct your students to walk into the side room one at a time and look at themselves in the mirror. Ask them to try to look at themselves as God would, sins and all. Then after taking an honest look at themselves, they can walk to the other table in the room and each take a drink of water to symbolize receiving the living water of God's grace.

Once students have finished, lead them in a few minutes of silent prayer and reflection about their experiences.

for younger teenagers

For a group of younger students, you or another adult leader might want to remain in the side room with them and guide them through the process to make sure they understand the significance of the activity. You could also modify the activity by using crayons and paper, prompting the students to sit at a table and each draw a picture of how God sees them.

leader tip

To facilitate the process, you can sing praise songs with the rest of the group while individuals get up to enter and exit the side room. If there are any teenagers in your group who are non-Christians or spiritual seekers, make it clear that what they do in the room is their own business. They don't have to drink the water or even enter the room if they are not ready.

leader tip

If your students or parents feel uncomfortable with the idea of drawing a temporary tattoo in "Student Quiet Time 2: Marked by Grace," then have students each draw the symbol in the center of a white handkerchief and tie it to their arms like armbands. If they feel uncomfortable sharing their symbols, they could wear them on the inside of their arms or folded against their skin.

small-group discussion 2

Discuss these questions in your small group:

• *Can you think of times when someone has confronted you with a truth you didn't want to hear? What happened? How did you react?*

• *When is it OK to tell a friend that you think he or she is making a mistake? How can you correct someone without condemning him or her?*

• *How can we stay open to the correcting voice of God?*

teaching session 4: living a grace-filled life

Ask your students to divide into groups of four. Have them read 2 Corinthians 9:8 and John 4:27-42, and then ask them how they think the Samaritan woman might have shared her faith with the people in her village. Ask each group to come up with a short skit detailing some ideas about how she might have effectively shared the message of God's grace with a villager or group of villagers. Give your students ten minutes to come up with skits, and then have each group present its skit to the larger group.

Once each group has presented its skit, ask: • **Did you have a hard time thinking about how the Samaritan woman may have explained grace to her fellow villagers? Why or why not?**

• **What obstacles do you think she might have encountered in telling her fellow villagers about Jesus?**

Summarize the end of the story by explaining that once the Samaritan woman was filled with God's grace, she felt compelled to share it with everyone she knew. Challenge students that as Christians, they have a similar responsibility to introduce others to grace. Prompt them to think of some concrete ways to show God's grace to others, just as the Samaritan woman showed grace to the people of her village.

List your teenagers' ideas on a poster board. Plan to take the poster back to the church with you and put it up in the youth room so that group members can start setting dates and goals to accomplish their ideas. After you have shared some more general ideas, ask students to form pairs and share ideas for personal applications of God's grace with each other. Then ask each person to pray for his or her partner.

STUDENT QUIET TIME 1: GOD'S GRACE MADE PERFECT IN WEAKNESS

(Instructions: Get a water-soluble marker and a cup of
water from your youth leader before you begin this quiet time.)

Just like the Samaritan woman, we all have sin in our lives. What sins would Jesus point out to you? Think about the sins that are interfering with your relationship with God. Try to concentrate on sins that might be particularly private or personal such as the Samaritan woman's sin of adultery. Use the marker to write all of the sins you come up with here.

Bow your head in prayer and ask God for forgiveness.

Read 2 Corinthians 12:7-9. We are all plagued with sinfulness and weakness. The good news is that God works through our weaknesses. Our sins are no match for the power of his grace!

When you are ready, dip your finger in water and then rub your finger over the sins you have just recorded until the words are blurred or erased from the paper. God's living water is enough to wash away your sins.

STUDENT QUIET TIME 2: MARKED BY GRACE

(Instructions: Get a permanent marker from your youth leader before you begin this quiet time.)

Sometimes we ignore the voice that offers us the goodness of grace by filling our lives with outside noise. Write about the ways you drown out the voice of God's grace in your life.

Read Hebrews 4:16. Think of ways you can boldly approach God's throne of grace. List these ideas and choose one symbol that sums up your resolution—perhaps a pair of folded hands to signify a renewed commitment to prayer, or a picture of something that is blocking your commitment to God, something you no longer want to rule your life. Picture that negative element with a cross or a jug of living water superimposed over it.

Take a permanent marker and draw the symbol on your skin. If you want it to be private, draw it on the inside of your ankle or the inside of your upper arm.

If your resolution isn't private, choose a partner, share your commitment, and ask him or her to help you keep it. You could even ask the person to draw your symbol for you as a further sign of your shared responsibility. Use your symbol as a reminder of your commitment in the days to come.

defeating doubt

retreat focus: Students will explore the relationship between faith and doubt by taking a closer look at the life of Thomas and several other Bible characters.

retreat motto: Believe in things you cannot see and see things you can't believe!

theme verse: "Look at the nations and watch—and be utterly amazed. For I am going to do something in your days that you would not believe, even if you were told" (Habakkuk 1:5).

preparation

Before the retreat, gather all of the necessary supplies and make all of the photocopies recommended in the Master Supply List.

For Teaching Session 1, cut paper into enough slips so that each student can have one.

For Teaching Session 2, cue up *October Sky* by setting the VCR counter at 0:00:00 when the studio logo appears before the movie starts. The segment you'll show starts at approximately 0:11:50 when Homer's friend says, "You can't be seen with him, Homer."

For Teaching Session 3, you'll also want to cue up *Indiana Jones and the Last Crusade* by setting the counter at 0:00:00 when the studio logo appears before the movie begins. Fast forward *Indiana Jones* to approximately 1:47:00 when Indiana approaches the edge of a cliff.

For Teaching Session 4, cue up *I.Q.* in the same manner, fast-forwarding to approximately 0:56:00 when James says, "Many of you may recognize this test."

Make sure students are divided into small groups (for more information on this, see p. 7), and take some time to study John 20 and Hebrews 11 on your own.

worship idea

For your theme song for the weekend, use "Open the Eyes of My Heart" from the two-CD set *I Could Sing of Your Love Forever*. For information on ordering student lyrics books, a song leader book, and the CDs, call Group at 1-800-447-1070.

---

leader tip

Avoid the embarrassment of showing the wrong scene— preview movie clips before using them!

---

master supply list

In addition to basic retreat supplies such as food, games, Bibles, pens, pencils, paper, and worship music, you'll also need the following supplies:

- ❏ 6 photocopies of the "The Hall of Faith" handout (p. 31)
- ❏ 1 can of Silly String for each small group
- ❏ 1 photocopy of "Small-Group Discussion 1" box (p. 23) for each small group
- ❏ 1 photocopy of "Student Quiet Time 1: How to Train an Elephant" (p. 29) for each student
- ❏ *October Sky* video (or DVD)
- ❏ VCR (or DVD player)
- ❏ TV
- ❏ flashlight
- ❏ *Indiana Jones and the Last Crusade* video (or DVD)
- ❏ 1 photocopy of "Small-Group Discussion 2" box (p. 26) for each small group
- ❏ blankets and lawn chairs
- ❏ CD player
- ❏ worship music CD
- ❏ 1 photocopy of "Student Quiet Time 2: Unhappy Endings" (p. 30) for each student
- ❏ *I.Q.* video (or DVD)
- ❏ binoculars
- ❏ optional: several black garbage bags, masking tape

suggested schedule

2-Night Retreat

Day	Time	Activity	Supplies
Friday	6:00-7:00 p.m.	Games	
	7:00-8:00 p.m.	Teaching Session 1: The Hall of Faith	Bibles, slips of paper, photocopies of "The Hall of Faith" handout (p. 31), pencils or pens
	8:00-9:15 p.m.	Free Time or Games	
	9:15-10:00 p.m.	Small-Group Discussion 1	Cans of Silly String, photocopies of "Small-Group Discussion 1" box (p. 23)
	10:00-10:30 p.m.	Snacks	
	11:00 p.m.	Lights Out	
Saturday	7:30-8:00 a.m.	Student Quiet Time 1: How to Train an Elephant	Bibles, photocopies of "Student Quiet Time 1: How to Train an Elephant" (p. 29), pencils or pens
	8:00-9:00 a.m.	Breakfast	
	9:00-10:00 a.m.	Teaching Session 2: Faith-Full Friends	Bibles, *October Sky* video, TV, VCR
	10:00-11:30 a.m.	Games or Group Activities	
	11:30 a.m.-12:30 p.m.	Lunch	
	12:30-5:00 p.m.	Free Time or Group Activities	
	5:00-6:00 p.m.	Dinner	
	6:00-7:00 p.m.	Games	
	7:00-7:45 p.m.	Teaching Session 3: Blackout	Bibles, flashlight, *Indiana Jones and the Last Crusade* video, TV, VCR Optional: trash bags and masking tape
	7:45-8:45 p.m.	Free Time	
	8:45-9:30 p.m.	Small-Group Discussion 2	Photocopies of "Small-Group Discussion 2" box (p. 26)
	9:30-10:00 p.m.	Worship Session: Under the Big Top	Bibles, blankets, lawn chairs, worship CD, CD player
	10:00-10:30 p.m.	Snacks	
	11:00 p.m.	Lights Out	
Sunday	7:30-8:00 a.m.	Student Quiet Time 2: Unhappy Endings	Bibles, photocopies of "Student Quiet Time 2: Unhappy Endings" (p. 30), pencils or pens
	8:00-9:00 a.m.	Breakfast	
	9:00-10:00 a.m.	Teaching Session 4: Father Knows Best	Bibles, paper, pencils or pens, TV, VCR, *I.Q.* video, binoculars
	10:00 a.m.-noon	Games or Group Activities	

1-Night Retreat

Day	Time	Activity	Supplies
Friday	6:00-7:15 p.m.	Games	
	7:15-8:15 p.m.	Teaching Session 1: The Hall of Faith	Bibles, slips of paper, photocopies of "The Hall of Faith" handout (p. 31), pencils or pens
	8:15-9:00 p.m.	Small-Group Discussion 1	Cans of Silly String, photocopies of "Small-Group Discussion 1" box (p. 23)
	9:00-9:30 p.m.	Worship Session: Under the Big Top	Bibles, blankets, lawn chairs, worship CD, CD player
	9:30-10:00 p.m.	Snacks	
	10:00-10:30 p.m.	Student Quiet Time 1: How to Train an Elephant	Bibles, photocopies of "Student Quiet Time 1: How to Train an Elephant" (p. 29), pencils or pens
	11:00 p.m.	Lights Out	
Saturday	7:30-8:00 a.m.	Student Quiet Time 2: Unhappy Endings	Bibles, photocopies of "Student Quiet Time 2: Unhappy Endings" (p. 30), pens or pencils
	8:00-9:00 a.m.	Breakfast	
	9:00-10:00 a.m.	Teaching Session 4: Father Knows Best	Bibles, paper, pencils or pens, TV, VCR, *I.Q.* video, binoculars
	10:00-11:30 a.m.	Games or Group Activities	
	11:30 a.m.-noon	Small-Group Discussion 2	Photocopies of "Small-Group Discussion 2" box (p. 26)

teaching session 1: the hall of faith

As teenagers arrive, distribute slips of paper and pens. Ask each participant to write down his or her most outrageous experience. This should be something that the other students would have a difficult time believing. If they can't think of anything zany enough, invite them to make something up. Collect the slips and randomly redistribute them. Then give students a chance to try and find the person who wrote the experience they received. Follow with a time of sharing, having students guess whether or not each experience really happened and providing opportunities for students to tell their true stories in greater detail.

Afterward, share some "unbelievable" stories of your own, then ask: • **Why are we sometimes skeptical about things that are out of the ordinary?**

• **Why do some things seem too good to be true?**

• **Do you feel skeptical about any particular Bible stories, Christian teachings, or ideas about God? Do you know others who do? What are some things you or others feel skeptical about when it comes to Christianity?**

Say: **Past experiences, unanswered prayer, trials, fear, and even human logic can sometimes chip away at our faith in God. The questions or doubts you might have about God, Christianity, or God's will for you are very normal and human. The Bible is filled with examples of people who felt the very same way when challenges arose.**

leader tip

You may want to begin each teaching session with five to ten minutes of singing. In addition to the suggested theme song, select other praise and worship songs that will complement the theme of the weekend.

Arrange students into six smaller groups (a group can be as small as one student if necessary). Distribute a copy of "The Hall of Faith" handout (p. 31) to each group, and assign each group one of the Bible characters listed in the left column. Explain that they should read the Scripture passage, discuss the story, and fill in that character's blanks on the chart. Groups should then brainstorm a brief and creative way to explain their character's story to everyone present.

for younger teenagers

Younger students might find it difficult to coordinate these small groups entirely on their own. Assign an adult leader to sit with each group, not to lead, but rather to support the group and keep the students on track.

After groups have finished their discussions, have them present their stories to the other students, then ask: • **How did these individuals deal with the questions and doubts they had about God and his will?**

• **In what ways did these individuals forfeit their own will for God's plan?**

• **Not all of these stories had happy endings. Why do you think the characters still held on to their faith?**

Invite a student to read Hebrews 11:1 aloud for the Bible's definition of faith, and assure teenagers that in the coming sessions they will study specific ways to deal with the questions and doubts that sometimes challenge their faith. Close by inviting a student to pray that God would help everyone present grow in his or her understanding of faith during the retreat.

small-group discussion 1

(Instructions: Get a can of Silly String from your youth leader before you begin this discussion.)

Work together in your small group to spray a spider web pattern on the ground with your Silly String. Spider webs appear delicate but are actually very tough—strong enough to carry big spiders and catch gigantic bugs. What makes them strong is their ability to stretch very far without breaking, like nylon.

When you've finished making your spider web, discuss these questions in your small group:

• How is faith similar to a spider web?

• Describe a time when your own faith was stretched or challenged. What were your feelings toward God during that time?

• How can we deal with those natural emotions and still please God in our response?

(Make sure you clean up the spider web afterward!)

teaching session 2: faith-full friends

To begin, ask teenagers to make an appropriate facial expression for each of the words you are about to say based on what they think each word means. Each word describes an emotion. Say the words one at a time, reading the definition after each one:

Melancholy (Depressed)

Incredulous (Skeptical)

Trepidation (Fear)

Arcane (Mysterious)

Ardent (Eager)

Ambivalent (Uncertain)

Zealous (Passionate)

Serene (Calm)

Ecstatic (Delighted)

Facetious (Silly)

Say: **Imagine the kind of emotions Jesus' disciples must have been dealing with after Jesus was killed. Only a week earlier, they were filled with anticipation as crowds celebrated Jesus as king. Almost overnight, all of their hopes and dreams were crushed. Jesus was betrayed by one of their closest friends, arrested, and killed. They had all left their homes and jobs to follow Jesus. Now he was gone, and they were left grieving, fearful, confused, and disappointed. Their faith was holding on by a thread.**

Ask a volunteer to read John 20:19-22 aloud. Say: **When their faith was put to the test, the disciples banded together. They found courage and faith through fellowship with one another.**

For a quick activity to help your teenagers understand that there is strength in numbers, ask half of them to form clusters of about ten students each. Ask two or three students to hug in the center of each cluster, and build the huddle around them, with other students clasping arms around the shoulders of their teammates as tightly as they can. Have the remaining students attempt to break up the existing huddles and pull teenagers away by loosening the grips they have around their teammates' shoulders.

After several minutes, whether or not they succeed, have students sit back down, and say: **One way the disciples dealt with faith challenges was by clinging to other Christians who were facing similar hardship. We can do the same by drawing on the comfort and strength of our Christian friends.**

Ask: • **Why do you think the disciples gathered together after Jesus was killed?**

• **What sorts of fears and feelings were they probably dealing with?**

• **How can Christian friends help pull you through times of doubt?**

Show a previewed clip from the movie *October Sky* beginning at approximately 0:11:50 when Homer's friend says, "You can't be seen with him, Homer." Stop the tape at approximately 0:17:25 when Homer's teacher says, "Have a good lunch, boys." Preface the clip by saying: **The movie *October Sky* is based on the true account of four friends who wanted desperately to overcome what most considered to be their fate—a life working underground in the town coal mine. None of the boys seemed extraordinary enough to forge a different path on his own, but when they joined forces, they defeated the odds by winning the science fair, college scholarships, and a ticket out of Coalwood. Throughout the movie, they are discouraged and criticized, but the boys are given the opportunity to do something spectacular with their lives because they relied on one another when obstacles arose.**

After the clip, close by saying: **Each of us faces challenges that test our faith. When those times come, don't feel you have to resolve those issues alone. Rely on your Christian friends to help pull you through.**

leader tip

Need game ideas? Check out the game book suggestions on page 7!

teaching session 3: blackout

You may want to prepare for the next teaching session by covering all of the windows in your meeting area with black trash bags. The lights should be turned off, making it as dark as possible. Use a flashlight to read.

As students sit in the dark, say: **Is it any wonder Thomas doubted? He had left his former life to follow a dreamer who spoke of a coming kingdom and told riddles that no one quite understood. His family must have thought he'd lost it when he quit his job to be a poverty-stricken "roadie." But things were just starting to look good. Jesus' popularity was soaring! The disciples' morale was at an all-time high.**

Then, life as he knew it was turned upside down.

Jesus was beaten, ridiculed, and killed. Thomas had seen Jesus perform miracles, even raise people from the dead! Why didn't Jesus do something? He left them looking like fools without a leader, their sense of purpose gone and their hopes crushed. Thomas had been cruelly disappointed.

If discouragement didn't challenge his faith, surely logic did. Jesus was dead and buried, end of story, right? No wonder he was skeptical when rumors surfaced that Jesus was alive. He wanted to see for himself, with his own two eyes. Wouldn't you?

Jesus wasn't angry or offended by Thomas' reaction. Jesus understood and was willing to give Thomas the answers he needed to believe.

Pass the flashlight to a student who'll read John 20:24-29 aloud.

Say: **Sometimes seeing is believing. Thomas saw the risen Christ and affirmed him immediately as Lord of his life. Doubts aren't necessarily bad. And when you have questions, it is never wrong to approach God seeking answers. However, there is also a special blessing that comes from blind faith—believing without seeing. Here in the darkened room, you may not be able to see more than a few feet around you. But the items and people in this meeting spot don't stop existing simply because you can't see them.**

Ask: • **Why is it difficult to believe in things we can't witness with our senses?**

• **How can you be sure of God's presence in your life?**

Show the video clip from *Indiana Jones and the Last Crusade* where Indiana takes a step onto the invisible bridge of faith. Begin at 1:47:00 when Indy approaches the cliff. End the clip at approximately 1:48:45 when Indy reaches the end of the bridge.

Ask: • **Have you ever felt like Indy? Like you've had to step out and take a big risk of faith? Explain.**

• **What are some faith-risks—unseeable or unprovable parts of faith like the bridge—that all Christians must accept as part of their belief?**

Say: **Faith is acting upon your belief even when you can't understand all of the**

for extra **impact**

Prior to teaching session 3, consider playing a game of blindfold Hide-and-Seek. You will need to clear out a wide-open playing space. Remove any obstacles since some participants will be blindfolded. Place students in teams of ten or twelve, and ask each team to select a meeting spot somewhere along the edge of the playing field. Choose one person from each group to stand in the center of the room. Give these designees each a blindfold which should be worn immediately. Next, ask the remaining teenagers to hide all over the room.

When they have selected their hiding spots, say: **When we begin, you should yell the name of your blindfolded teammate to help him or her find you. When you are found, go to your team's designated meeting spot while the blindfolded teammate continues to search.** Continue the game until all teenagers have returned to their meeting spots.

As the game finishes and students prepare for worship, ask them to consider how they feel when they can't see what's in front of them. Encourage them to think about how those same feelings apply to their spiritual situation.

evidence or see the outcome. Just as you can't always rely on your senses to determine reality, you can't always see what God has in mind. His plans go beyond the limits of human intellect. When you face a struggle that seems to crush you, or if believing in God just doesn't seem to make sense anymore, approach him for answers and keep believing. "Blessed are those who have not seen and yet have believed."

---

small-group discussion 2

Work together to create human stilts. Two people should each hold one leg of a third person and attempt to walk that person around a small area. Be careful!

After everyone in your group has had a turn, discuss these questions:

· How might Christian friendships be like the human stilts, carrying you through times of doubt or uncertainty?

· How can you be a friend to someone who is struggling in his or her faith?

· What are some ways to approach God with doubts and concerns?

· Can doubting and searching strengthen your faith? Why or why not?

---

worship session: under the big top

Lead teenagers outside and stand in a circle. Explain to the students that in times of doubt, one simple way to strengthen their faith is to observe nature as a reminder that God is real.

Invite a student to read Romans 1:19-20 aloud. Ask: • **How can you see God's presence in the natural world?**

Go around the circle and invite each teenager to give one specific example.

Provide blankets and lawn chairs and encourage students to spread out and enjoy the night sky, taking some time to simply remember that God is in heaven and is in control.

Play a worship CD in the background, or sing worship songs to conclude the time outside.

teaching session 4: father knows best

Distribute paper and pencils as students enter the meeting area, and inform them that there will be a pop quiz. To begin, show the clip from *I.Q.* beginning at approximately 0:56:00 when James says, "Many of you may recognize this test." Stop the clip at approximately 1:00:45 when Ed says, "I'm done. Is that it?"

Next, ask your students the following trivia questions. They should write their answers on the paper provided.

• **In the thirty-ninth year of this king's reign, he came down with a foot disease that claimed his life the next year. Who was this king of Judah?**

A. Jehoshaphat

B. Asa

C. Ahab

D. Henry VIII

(Answer: B, 2 Chronicles 16:12-13)

• **This man threw rocks and dirt at King David and his troops, cursing David as they rode by. David spared the man's life and he wasn't punished. Why was this man angry with David?**

A. David was trespassing on his land.

B. The man liked giants.

C. He was a friend of Saul's family.

D. David sent this man's son into battle.

(Answer: C, 2 Samuel 16:5-8)

• **In the book of Revelation, the Lamb opens seven seals. What appears when the second seal is opened?**

A. A white horse

B. A black horse

C. A red horse

D. A talking horse

(Answer: C, Revelation 6:4)

After they have completed the test and you have shared the correct answers, say: **Do you ever feel like the whole point behind classes like trigonometry is to show you just how much you don't know? Sometimes it seems like the more we learn, the more we find there is to learn. That's one reason why God asks us to trust him since he knows so much more than we do. It's a little like when you were a kid and your parents asked you to do things that you didn't always understand.**

Ask: • **What are some of the rules or instructions your parents gave you as a child that didn't seem to make much sense?**

• **How did you feel about the rules at the time?**

• **How do you feel about the rules now?**

Say: **Usually, parents have the best interests of their children in mind, and we avoid a lot of trouble by trusting their advice. We can benefit from the wisdom of their experience. That's the way it is with God. He understands so much better than we do and can see the big picture. Still, that's hard to remember when we encounter hardships.**

Ask a volunteer to read Habakkuk 1:2-4 aloud. Say: **Habakkuk was addressing God on behalf of the people. They needed help, and God seemed to be taking his time. Habakkuk's faith was being stretched as he waited for God's justice and intervention. God's reply wasn't angry or condescending.**

Invite a student to read Habakkuk 1:5 aloud. Say: **God had a plan and he challenged Habakkuk to simply trust. God was doing something that was beyond the scope of Habakkuk's mental horizon or imagination. The passage continues and God told Habakkuk in chapter 2 verse 4, "The righteous will live by his faith."**

Invite a student to look out of a window in your meeting space and describe what he or she sees. Then give the student a pair of binoculars and have him or her look out of the window again, describing for the others his or her new perspective. When the student has finished, pass the binoculars around.

Say: **God could see something that Habakkuk could not, and he asked Habakkuk to keep believing.**

Each person we have studied this weekend had something in common. In each case, God had a plan in mind that the people couldn't understand, and it was dependent on their faith to carry it out. Faith is believing, despite the challenges that arise, that God knows best and cares about you.

Ask: • **What are some faith challenges that teenagers face on a regular basis?**

• **What faith challenges are you facing personally?**

• **How will you protect your faith when those obstacles arise?**

To close, say: **In the coming years, there will be many challenges to your faith. They may come in the form of a teacher who laughs at the very existence of God. Friends might tease you for your belief or convictions. You might face heartbreak, even the loss of someone dear to you. When your faith feels like a thin thread and you are clutching on to it for dear life, just remember that God's hand is right underneath you like a safety net—remember that he has a plan.**

Student Quiet Time 1:

How to Train an Elephant

Picture an elephant in captivity. At a young age, the elephant is shackled and cannot break free. The elephant grows and occasionally tugs at its constraints, but feels the resistance and gives up. The full-grown elephant never realizes its own strength. Its spirit is broken. The elephant is held by a rope it could *easily* break and is bossed around a circus ring by a man wearing spandex, never knowing it could actually pop the tiny guy in its mouth like a french fry.

We often live the same way, never realizing our potential because we are convinced of our limitations. In contrast, the Bible teaches there is nothing that can hold us back if we have even the smallest amount of real faith. Nothing is impossible. Never be convinced that you are less than you are. (And *never* wear spandex.)

Read Matthew 17:20.

• What sort of faith does this verse describe? Faith in what?

• What things are holding you back from your fullest faith potential?

• How does faith make it possible to do things you never imagined?

Student Quiet Time 2:
unhappy endings

Once there lived a beautiful princess who came across a talking frog. "Kiss Me," he said. "If you do, a spell will be broken and I will be transformed into a handsome prince."

Eventually she was persuaded. She closed her eyes and gave the frog a smooch. To her disappointment, the frog was still a frog. "Hey, I thought you were a handsome prince," said the annoyed princess.

"I thought you were a good kisser," replied the frog.

We aren't always guaranteed a happy ending. John the Baptist had proclaimed Jesus as Messiah. Jesus heralded John as the greatest person to ever live. Yet, John was imprisoned for preaching God's message. Doubt and despair rattled even *his* rock-solid faith. He sent his disciples to Jesus for answers and he got reassurance, but not relief. He was eventually beheaded in prison. Jesus' words encouraged him to the end: "Blessed is the man who does not fall away."

Read Matthew 11:2-6.

• Why does God sometimes not rescue us?

• How can faith in God survive those times when God or circumstances seem to make no sense?

• What blessing does God promise to those who live by faith?

The Hall of Faith

Directions: Work in teams to complete the chart for the character you have been assigned. Then brainstorm a creative way to present your character's story to the entire group.

WHO	Challenge	*Feelings*	RESPONSE	Result
Mary and Martha John 11:17-44	Death of brother	How could you let this happen, Jesus?		
Abraham Genesis 22:1-18	Loss of only son		I have no idea why you want this, God, but I'll obey.	
Job Job 1:6-22	Loss of children and possessions, troubled marriage, illness			God rewards Job with more than he had before.
John the Baptist Matthew 11:2-11; 14:3-10	Imprisonment and execution	Are you really who you claim to be, Jesus?		
The Twelve Spies Numbers 13:25—14:9	A fearsome battle		Ten chickened out, but two believed.	
Shadrach, Meshach, and Abednego Daniel 3:1-28	Death		Even if you don't save me, I'll still do what is right.	

gifts given for his glory

master supply list

In addition to basic retreat supplies such as food, games, Bibles, pens, pencils, paper, and worship music, you'll need the following supplies:

- ❏ 1 roll of wrapping paper for every four students
- ❏ index cards
- ❏ tape
- ❏ ribbon
- ❏ 1 photocopy of "Small-Group Discussion 1" box (p. 35) for each small group
- ❏ 1 feather for each student
- ❏ 1 photocopy of "Student Quiet Time 1: Just Like the Wind" (p. 40) for each student
- ❏ about a dozen children's puzzles (12-piece or less)
- ❏ newsprint
- ❏ black markers
- ❏ 1 photocopy of "The Gifts" handout (p. 42) for approximately every fifteen students
- ❏ 1 photocopy of "Small-Group Discussion 2" box (p. 38) for each small group
- ❏ 1 photocopy of "Student Quiet Time 2: No Take-Backs" (p. 41) for each student
- ❏ 1 small rock for each student
- ❏ 1 photocopy of "The Impact" box (p. 39) for each group of three or four students
- ❏ optional: bucket or plastic wading pool

retreat focus: Students will investigate what the Bible has to say about spiritual gifts and will consider Timothy's example of fanning his gifts into flame.

retreat motto: Gifted for a purpose

theme verse: "For this reason I remind you to fan into flame the gift of God, which is in you through the laying on of my hands. For God did not give us a spirit of timidity, but a spirit of power, of love and of self-discipline" (2 Timothy 1:6-7).

preparation

Before the retreat, gather all of the necessary supplies and make all of the photocopies recommended in the Master Supply List.

For Teaching Session 1, unwrap the wrapping paper from the rolls, write out 2 Timothy 1:6-7 on several index cards, and tape them to the cardboard rolls. Wrap the wrapping paper back over the rolls.

For Teaching Session 2, pick out a local ministry such as your church, a local homeless shelter, or something similar that is large enough for students to analyze. At the top of a large piece of newsprint, write the name of the ministry you've chosen.

For Teaching Session 3, cut apart the photocopies of "The Gifts" handout (p. 42).

For Teaching Session 4, if your retreat area is not near a lake or pond, fill a large bucket or plastic wading pool with water.

Make sure students are divided into small groups (for more information on this, see p. 7), and take some time to study Romans 12:6-8; 1 Corinthians 12:8-10, 28-30; Ephesians 4:11; and 1 Peter 4:9-11 on your own.

worship idea

For your theme song for the weekend, use "Joy" from the two-CD set *I Could Sing of Your Love Forever.* For information on ordering student lyrics books, a song leader book, and the CDs, call Group at 1-800-447-1070.

suggested schedule

2-Night Retreat

Day	Time	Activity	Supplies
Friday	6:00-7:00 p.m.	Games	
	7:00-8:00 p.m.	Teaching Session 1: The Best Gift Ever	Bibles, rolls of wrapping paper, tape, ribbon, index cards, pens or pencils
	8:00-9:30 p.m.	Free Time or Games	
	9:30-10:00 p.m.	Small-Group Discussion 1	Photocopies of "Small-Group Discussion 1" box (p. 35)
	10:00-10:30 p.m.	Snacks	
	11:00 p.m.	Lights Out	
Saturday	7:30-8:00 a.m.	Student Quiet Time 1: Just Like the Wind	Bibles, photocopies of "Student Quiet Time 1: Just Like the Wind" (p. 40), feathers, pens or pencils
	8:00-9:00 a.m.	Breakfast	
	9:00-10:30 a.m.	Games or Group Activities	
	10:30-11:30 a.m.	Teaching Session 2: One Body, Many Parts	Bibles, children's puzzles, newsprint, markers
	11:30 a.m.-12:30 p.m.	Lunch	
	12:30-4:30 p.m.	Free Time	
	4:30-5:30 p.m.	Dinner	
	5:30-6:30 p.m.	Games or Group Activities	
	6:30-7:30 p.m.	Teaching Session 3: The Gifts	Bibles, photocopies of "The Gifts" handout (p. 42), paper, pens or pencils, newsprint, marker
	7:30-9:30 p.m.	Free Time	
	9:30-10:00 p.m.	Small-Group Discussion 2	Photocopies of "Small-Group Discussion 2" box (p. 38)
	10:00-10:30 p.m.	Snacks	
	11:00 p.m.	Lights Out	
Sunday	7:30-8:00 a.m.	Student Quiet Time 2: No Take-Backs	Bibles, photocopies of "Student Quiet Time 2: No Take-Backs" (p. 41), pens or pencils
	8:00-9:00 a.m.	Breakfast	
	9:00-10:30 a.m.	Games or Group Activities	
	10:30 a.m.-noon	Teaching Session 4: The Impact	Bibles, small rocks, black markers, photocopies of "The Impact" box (p. 39) Optional: bucket or wading pool

Day	Time	Activity	Supplies
Friday	6:00-7:00 p.m.	Games	
	7:00-8:00 p.m.	Teaching Session 2: One Body, Many Parts	Bibles, children's puzzles, newsprint, markers
	8:00-9:00 p.m.	Games or Group Activities	
	9:00-10:00 p.m.	Teaching Session 3: The Gifts	Bibles, photocopies of "The Gifts" handout (p. 42), pens or pencils, paper, newsprint, marker
	10:00-10:30 p.m.	Small-Group Discussion 1	Photocopies of "Small-Group Discussion 1" box (p. 35)
	11:00 p.m.	Lights Out	
Saturday	7:30-8:00 a.m.	Student Quiet Time 1: Just Like the Wind	Bibles, photocopies of "Student Quiet Time 1: Just Like the Wind" (p. 40), feathers, pens or pencils
	8:00-9:00 a.m.	Breakfast	
	9:00-10:30 a.m.	Teaching Session 4: The Impact	Bibles, small rocks, black markers, photocopies of "The Impact" box (p. 39) Optional: bucket or wading pool
	10:30 a.m.-noon	Games or Group Activities	

leader tip

You may want to begin each teaching session with five to ten minutes of singing. In addition to the suggested theme song, select other praise and worship songs that will complement the theme of the weekend.

teaching session 1: the best gift ever

Begin the session by having students form groups of four and giving each group a roll of wrapping paper, ribbon, and tape.

Say: **Think back to the best gift you ever got. It could have been for your birthday, Christmas, or for no reason at all. It could have been a puppy, an air hockey game, a bicycle, or something not material—a Christmas when your brother was able to come home for the holidays, for example. Take a few moments and think of that favorite gift.**

Next, instruct students to create their own mini-sculptures of their favorite gifts using the supplies given. For example, if someone's favorite gift was a puppy one Christmas, he or she will create the shape of a puppy using the paper, ribbon, and tape by crumpling, tying, and taping. When students have finished, have them share in their groups what their sculptures represent and why they chose them as their favorite gifts.

for younger teenagers

Instead of having your younger teenagers "sculpt" their favorite gifts, consider having them do a more active game instead, such as charades. Groups could have each person act out his or her favorite gift while the others in the group try to guess what it is. (You may need adult volunteers to help with the groups.)

Ask: • **How did you feel when you got the gifts represented here?**

• **How do you think the givers felt when they gave them to you?**

• **What gifts does God give to us?**

• **What are we supposed to do with his gifts to us?**

Direct students' attention to the wrapping paper core, and have one person in each group read the verses aloud within their group. Then have students discuss the following questions in their groups:

• **What do you think spiritual gifts are and why does God give them?**

• **What can we do with our spiritual gifts?**

Ask groups to share their responses with the other groups. After all groups have done so, have them join back together.

Say: **We give gifts because we love the people we're giving them to. With God it's the same way. God loves us and gives us spiritual gifts. But he wants *us* to give as well, by using our gifts to bring others closer to him. He also gives us gifts so we can serve the church, working together to achieve its ministry goals. Just as you unrolled the wrapping paper and discovered a Scripture passage on the core, God wants the "core" of what we do to be motivated by our love and service to God.**

On this retreat, we're going to learn about spiritual gifts, what they are, and what we should do with them. Just as Timothy was instructed by Paul to "fan into flame" his spiritual gifts, we are expected to seek out and use our gifts to bring glory to God and to fulfill his purpose for us.

small-group discussion 1

Discuss the following questions in your small group:

· *Why does God give us spiritual gifts?*

· *Why do you think we don't all have the same spiritual gifts?*

· *Name as many spiritual gifts as you can.*

· *Think of someone you know who uses his or her spiritual gifts. What are that person's gifts and how does he or she use them?*

teaching session 2: one body, many parts

Tape the large piece of newsprint with the name of the ministry you've chosen in a prominent place in the room. Gather the children's puzzles together in three piles in the front of the room for the opening activity.

Begin the session by having students form three groups. Have each group form its own line at the end of the room opposite the puzzles. The objective of the game is to have teams work together to see how many puzzles they can collectively put together in five minutes. When you yell "go," the first person from each team will run to the puzzles, take the top puzzle, spill out and mess up the pieces, and put the puzzle back together (they can do this on the floor). On finishing the puzzle, he or she will put it back into the box, shake the box, put it on the bottom of the stack, run back to the team, tag the next person in line, then go to the back of the line. It's OK if students take multiple turns. Keep track of the number of puzzles the groups put together, and when the time is up, congratulate all three teams on their ability to work together quickly to assemble that many puzzles.

Ask: • **Have any of you ever put together a bigger puzzle with, say, one thousand pieces? What's the highest number of pieces you've ever worked with and completed?**

Say: **Sometimes the most frustrating thing about putting together a huge puzzle is the fact that all the pieces are different. You might spend hours looking for just one piece to fit one particular spot. But we also know that if many of the pieces were the same, we couldn't complete the puzzle. They have to be different in order to make the whole picture work.**

Have a volunteer read aloud 1 Corinthians 12:18-20.

Ask: • **If a human body was made up of only one or two body parts, how would that affect the way it functions?**

• **How is this similar to putting together a puzzle?**

• **What does God mean by "the body" in this passage?**

Say: **When we become Christians, we become a part of the body of God's people who all work together to accomplish his purpose on earth, using the spiritual gifts we've been given. Let's look at an example of a place where many different gifts are needed for ministry.**

Direct students' attention to the ministry name on the piece of newsprint and say: **Let's identify the many different roles involved in the work that's being done at the ministry listed here.**

List all their responses on the newsprint.

Ask: • **How do these different roles work together? Give me an example of two or three that work together.**

• **Why is it necessary to have people with different gifts involved in the same project?**

• **Is it possible to rate spiritual gifts in order of importance? Why or why not?**

Say: **God gives us different spiritual gifts so that we can cover the many different areas needed to complete the big picture he's enlisted us to help with. We**

leader tip

Need game ideas? Check out the game book suggestions on page 7!

are all an important part of God's work, and we are each chosen by him to exercise certain gifts. Since we need all the gifts, no one is more needed or more important than the other—we are *all* vital to God's work.

teaching session 3: the gifts

Begin the session by having students form groups of three or four. Distribute the slips from "The Gifts" handout you prepared so that each group has an approximately equal number of slips. Also pass out Bibles, pens, and paper to each group. Instruct each group to read the explanations of the gifts and to study the Scriptures in their Bibles, then challenge them to write out one specific example of a way a teenager could live out each of the different gifts they've studied.

Give them fifteen to twenty minutes to complete this assignment. When they've finished, have groups present their gifts and the examples they came up with. As they read the gifts, write them on a large piece of newsprint taped in a prominent place where everyone can see.

Say: **Many theologians agree that the lists of spiritual gifts in the Bible are not exhaustive, meaning there are probably way more than what you see here. While we don't know for certain what those are, know that you can use your talents and abilities to minister to others and do God's work. So in addition to seeking out your gifts, think about your talents and abilities that can be used by God.**

Have a volunteer read Acts 16:1-5, then say: **This passage is a great example of a young person using his gifts where he was. Timothy is described as a "disciple," and those who knew him and his ministry work "spoke well of him" to Paul. We can assume that Timothy was using his spiritual gifts in the town where he lived before he joined Paul on his journey, a journey that probably changed not only Timothy's life, but also the lives of countless others.**

Pass out paper to each student. Have a brief time of silence and ask them to consider what gift or gifts they think God may have given them and write them on the paper. As they think about their gifts, have them close their eyes and pray silently, asking God to help them discern what their gifts are and how to use them.

small-group discussion 2

Discuss these questions in your small group:

• How is being a member of the body of people doing God's work similar to being on a sports team? How is it different?

• What would your response be to people who might feel they weren't gifted at anything?

• What things do you enjoy that might indicate a spiritual gift?

• Share what you think your spiritual gift or gifts might be, and one experience with trying out that gift that helped you recognize it in your life.

teaching session 4: the impact

Begin the session by taking your group out to a calm body of water, such as a river, lake, or pond (or using a bucket or wading pool filled with water).

Say: **For this retreat, we've focused on spiritual gifts—what they are, what we've been gifted with, and what we should do with our gifts. Now we're going to consider the effects using our gifts can have on others.**

Have students form groups of three. Give each group a Bible and a copy of "The Impact" box (p. 39). Have one volunteer from each group read aloud 1 Timothy 4:12-14, then have students discuss the questions within their groups. Ask a few to share their groups' responses if there's time.

Pass out a rock to each person and a black marker to each group. Ask everyone to think of one word, letter, or symbol that represents a specific spiritual gift of theirs, and have them each write it on their rock.

Next, have students come back together as one big group. Take a few minutes to share a personal story of a person who had an impact on you, who used his or her spiritual gifts and affected your life in a positive way.

Ask: • **Now I'd love to hear from you. Do you know people who affected you in a positive way? Did they use their spiritual gifts to do that? Tell us about those people.**

After several students have shared, say: **The effect you have on someone can be life-changing, and it doesn't stop there. It's like the ripples that are created when you toss a rock in the water.** (Toss your rock into the water.) **The rock creates a ripple, and then another ripple, and so on. Using your spiritual gifts for God will have far-reaching positive effects on others. God has uniquely equipped you! Just** imagine how much you can do.

Tell students you're going to have a time of silence. Instruct them to each come to the water, one by one, toss their rock in, and watch the ripples.

Say: **As you watch the ripples extend out, say a silent prayer asking God to help you use your gifts to be a positive example to others.**

When everyone has had a turn, form a circle and hold hands. Say: **Don't forget everything you've learned during this retreat. Take it with you and use it to help others. You are all uniquely gifted. You all have very important gifts to use and give back to God by giving to others.**

Close with a prayer thanking God for his gifts and asking for guidance as you seek to express those gifts in your life.

---

the impact

Read 1 Timothy 4:12-14.

· *Why does Paul tell Timothy to set an example by the way he lives his life?*

· *Why is it so important to not neglect our spiritual gifts?*

· *What's one way that using your gift can have a positive impact on someone else?*

STUDENT QUIET TIME 1: Just Like the Wind

(*Instructions:* Get a feather from your youth leader before you begin this quiet time.)

Find a quiet spot outside where you can observe nature. If the weather's bad, find a spot inside near a window, or just use your imagination.

Put your feather close to your mouth. Take a breath, blow, and let go of the feather. How does it respond?

Sit quietly for a moment. Is a breeze blowing? How is nature responding to the wind? So much of nature responds by "giving"—leaves rustle, stems bow, branches move however the wind directs. They don't all respond the same way, but they are all affected by the wind.

Read 1 Corinthians 12:4-6. Just as nature responds in different ways to the wind, we are all asked to use our unique spiritual gifts to do different things as a response to the power of God's Spirit in our lives. We should always respond to God by giving in to his direction for us. Our gifts may be different, but they all come from the same God.

• How is God like the wind?

• What should your response be to God's moving in your life? Why?

• In the different kinds of working we do, what should be the one constant reason for our work? Why?

Student Quiet Time 2:
No Take-Backs

Think about some nonmaterial gifts you've received that would never be taken back by the giver, such as parental love, a happy childhood memory, or special recognition you received for a job well done.

Read Romans 11:29. God chose certain gifts for you, and he has plans for your gifts to be used to help achieve his purpose for his people on earth.

God believes in you and knows you can accomplish his work with those gifts. He is confident that you can put them to their best use. While that's exciting, it's also a big responsibility. God gives us spiritual gifts with the understanding that we won't hide them—we'll *use* them. Yes, it's work—but it's the most rewarding work you'll ever do.

• How does it make you feel to know that God has chosen to give you your unique gifts for a specific purpose?

• You can respond in two ways to God's leading to use your gifts: yes or no. What could happen if you said yes? What could happen if you said no?

• How can you live out saying yes to using your spiritual gifts?

THE GIFTS

INSTRUCTIONS: Cut along the dotted lines and pass out several of the gifts to each group. These gifts are mentioned in the following Scriptures: Romans 12:6-8; 1 Corinthians 12:8-10, 28-30; Ephesians 4:11; and 1 Peter 4:9-11. *(Feel free to modify this activity by leaving out any of the gifts that you feel aren't congruent with your church's traditions.)*

Serving—Recognizing practical needs and working to meet them and provide support. (Scriptural example: Luke 7:36-50)

Teaching—Educating others about the truths of God's Word in such a way that encourages growth. (Scriptural example: Nehemiah 8:1-18)

Encouraging—Lifting up others through speaking words of comfort and inspiration. (Scriptural example: Acts 11:22-24)

Giving—Contributing generously whatever resources are needed. (Scriptural example: Acts 4:32-35)

Leadership—Directing people as they do God's work in a manner that is strong and effective. (Scriptural example: Exodus 10:3; 12:31-32)

Showing Mercy—Having compassion for and helping those who are hurting. (Luke 10:25-37)

Wisdom—Helping others see how God's truth is applicable to issues and problems. (Scriptural example: 1 Kings 3:7-14)

Knowledge—Understanding and explaining biblical truths. (Scriptural example: Acts 18:24-28)

Faith—Having and living out confidence in God's promises. (Scriptural example: Hebrews 11:8-16)

Discernment—Having the ability to see motivations and distinguishing the truth or falsehood of something. (Scriptural example: 1 Kings 3:16-27)

Apostleship—Seeing a need and being able to start new ministries. (Scriptural example: Acts 20:17-24)

Administration—Organizing the parts of ministry to bring about more effective ministry work. (Scriptural example: Acts 6:1-7)

Evangelism—Speaking the message of Jesus' love in a way that draws others to new faith in him. (Scriptural example: John 1:6-9, 19-28)

Hospitality—The ability to welcome others and make them feel comfortable, especially if they are strangers to your environment. (Scriptural example: Acts 16:11-15)

Prophecy—Communicating the gospel in a way that helps us see our sin and leads to repentance. (Scriptural example: Jeremiah 1:4-9, 17-19)

Tongues—Speaking or praying in a language that is unknown to the speaker. (Scriptural example: Acts 2:1-4)

Interpretation of Tongues—Understanding and translating the message of someone who is speaking in tongues. (Scriptural example: 1 Corinthians 14:26-28)

Miracles—The ability to bring about glory to God through supernatural acts. (Scriptural example: Acts 5:12-16)

Healing—Being used by God to help bring health (physical, mental, or otherwise) to people. (Scriptural example: Acts 3:1-10)

the kingdom of surprises

retreat focus: Students will investigate Jesus' teachings in the Sermon on the Mount and will consider how they can reflect the values of God's kingdom in their own lives.

retreat motto: Stop chasing happiness and let God find you.

theme verse: "Seek first his kingdom and his righteousness, and all these things will be given to you as well" (Matthew 6:33).

preparation

Before the retreat, gather all of the necessary supplies and make all of the photocopies recommended in the Master Supply List.

For Teaching Session 1, write the words "Happy are…" in the middle of a piece of poster board. On another, smaller piece of poster board, write the words "Blessed are…"

For Teaching Session 2, write each of the following Beatitude qualities and Bible story references on its own index card:

- Poor in spirit: Woman subject to bleeding (Matthew 9:20-22)

- Mourning: Mary and Martha (John 11:1-44)

- Meekness: Children in the kingdom (Matthew 18:1-5)

- Hunger and thirst: Zacchaeus (Luke 19:1-10)

- Mercy: The forgiving king (Matthew 18:21-35)

- Pure in heart: Simeon (Luke 2:22-35)

- Peacemakers: Peter (Acts 11:1-18)

- Persecuted: Paul and Silas (Acts 16:16-34)

For Teaching Session 3, cut a large piece of poster board into nine interlocking jigsaw pieces. Use a pencil to write one of the following Scripture references on each piece: Matthew 13:24-30; Matthew 13:31-32; Matthew 13:33; Matthew 13:44; Matthew 13:45-46; Matthew 13:47-50; Matthew 18:23-35; Matthew 20:1-16; Matthew 22:1-14.

For Teaching Session 4, cue up the *Mission Impossible* video by setting the VCR counter at 0:00:00 when the studio logo appears before the movie starts. The segment you'll show starts at approximately 0:04:05 when the flight attendant asks Jim Phelps if he'd like to watch a movie. Also, on several index cards, write out one or two lines of

master supply list

In addition to basic retreat supplies such as food, games, Bibles, pens, pencils, paper, and worship music, you'll also need the following supplies:

- ❏ 2 CD players
- ❏ 2 CDs of different styles of music
- ❏ several pairs of scissors
- ❏ several magazines and newspapers
- ❏ 5 pieces of poster board
- ❏ several glue sticks
- ❏ markers
- ❏ 1 photocopy of "Small-Group Discussion 1" box (p. 47) for each small group
- ❏ 1 photocopy of "Student Quiet Time 1: Expectations" (p. 52) for each student
- ❏ index cards
- ❏ basic art supplies such as crayons, markers, colored pencils, glitter, construction paper, paints, paintbrushes, and glue
- ❏ 3 bowls
- ❏ several dictionaries
- ❏ 1 picture of each student *or* an instant-print camera and film (or a digital camera with a computer, printer, and photo quality paper)
- ❏ 1 photocopy of "Small-Group Discussion 2" box (p. 50) for each small group
- ❏ 1 photocopy of "Student Quiet Time 2: Don't Worry!" (p. 53) for each student
- ❏ 1 piece of string (about 9 to 12 inches long) for each student

(continued on p. 44)

(continued from p. 43)

- ❏ TV
- ❏ VCR (or DVD player)
- ❏ *Mission: Impossible* video (or DVD)
- ❏ salt
- ❏ flashlight
- ❏ salty snacks (such as salted nuts or potato chips)
- ❏ 1 large candle
- ❏ several small candles
- ❏ matches
- ❏ flip chart
- ❏ optional: tropical drinks and fruits

challenging scenarios that your students are likely to encounter at school, at church, or at home. For example, you could write situations such as:

• A friend is very upset because she has had an argument with her mom.

• A friend is laughing about someone you know who goes to your church. He says, "He's such a nerd—why are all Christians such losers?"

• A friend uses Jesus' name as a swear word and then looks at you, expecting you to protest. What do you say?

Make sure students are divided into small groups (for more information on this, see p. 7), and take some time to study Jesus' entire Sermon on the Mount in Matthew 5–7 on your own.

leader tip

Avoid the embarrassment of showing the wrong scene— preview movie clips before using them!

worship idea

For your theme song for the weekend, use "Did You Feel the Mountains Tremble?" from the two-CD set *I Could Sing of Your Love Forever*. For information on ordering student lyrics books, a song leader book, and the CDs, call Group at 1-800-447-1070.

suggested schedule

2-Night Retreat

Day	Time	Activity	Supplies
Friday	6:00-7:00 p.m.	Games	
	7:00-8:00 p.m.	Teaching Session 1: Happy Are…	Bibles, 2 CD players, CDs, poster board, newspapers, magazines, glue, markers, paper
	8:00-9:30 p.m.	Free Time or Games	
	9:30-10:00 p.m.	Small-Group Discussion 1	Photocopies of "Small-Group Discussion 1" box (p. 47)
	10:00-10:30 p.m.	Snacks	
	11:00 p.m.	Lights Out	
Saturday	7:30-8:00 a.m.	Student Quiet Time 1: Expectations	Bibles, photocopies of "Student Quiet Time 1: Expectations" (p. 52), pencils or pens
	8:00-9:00 a.m.	Breakfast	
	9:00-10:00 a.m.	Games	
	10:00-11:30 a.m.	Teaching Session 2: Surprising Blessings	Bibles, paper, bowl, pens, dictionaries, index cards, art supplies (crayons, paints, collage materials)
	11:30 a.m.-12:30 p.m.	Lunch	
	12:30-6:00 p.m.	Free Time or Group Activities	
	6:00-7:00 p.m.	Dinner	
	7:00-8:30 p.m.	Teaching Session 3: Secret Agents	Bibles; paper; poster board; pens; art supplies (markers, crayons, paints); a photo of each student or an instant-print camera or a digital camera, computer, and printer Optional: tropical drinks and exotic fruits
	8:30-9:30 p.m.	Free Time	
	9:30-10:00 p.m.	Small-Group Discussion 2	Photocopies of "Small-Group Discussion 2" box (p. 50)
	10:00-10:30 p.m.	Snacks	
	11:00 p.m.	Lights Out	
Sunday	7:30-8:00 a.m.	Student Quiet Time 2: Don't Worry!	Bibles, photocopies of "Student Quiet Time 2: Don't Worry!" (p. 53), pieces of string, pencils or pens
	8:00-9:00 a.m.	Breakfast	
	9:00-10:30 a.m.	Teaching Session 4: Mission Impossible?	Bibles, TV, VCR, *Mission: Impossible* video, poster board, flashlight, salt, pens, flip chart, index cards, salty snacks, large candle, small candles, matches
	10:30 a.m.-noon	Games or Group Activities	

Day	Time	Activity	Supplies
Friday	6:00-7:00 p.m.	Games	
	7:00-8:00 p.m.	Teaching Session 1: Happy Are…	Bibles, 2 CD players, CDs, poster board, newspapers, magazines, glue, markers, paper
	8:00-9:30 p.m.	Free Time	
	9:30-10:00 p.m.	Snacks	
	10:00-10:30 p.m.	Small-Group Discussion 1	Photocopies of "Small-Group Discussion 1" box (p. 47)
	11:00 p.m.	Lights Out	
Saturday	7:30-8:00 a.m.	Student Quiet Time 1: Expectations	Bibles, photocopies of "Student Quiet Time 1: Expectations" (p. 52), pencils or pens
	8:00-9:00 a.m.	Breakfast	
	9:30-10:00 a.m.	Small-Group Discussion 2	Photocopies of "Small-Group Discussion 2" box (p. 50)
	10:00-10:30 a.m.	Games	
	10:30 a.m.-noon	Teaching Session 4: Mission Impossible?	Bibles, TV, VCR, *Mission: Impossible* video, poster board, flashlight, salt, bowl, pens, flip chart, index cards, salty snacks, large candle, small candles, matches

leader tip

You may want to begin each teaching session with five to ten minutes of singing. In addition to the suggested theme song, select other praise and worship songs that will complement the theme of the weekend.

teaching session 1: happy are…

Begin by setting up two CD players and playing two different CDs at the same time. After a few minutes, say: **No one plays two different kinds of music at the same time—you aren't able to enjoy either properly. But when it comes to hearing messages about what's important in life from society, church, or our families, we often have to listen to different things at the same time, and work out which is right.**

Ask: • **Can anyone think of an example of two different messages that the church and the world give about the same thing?**

Ask students to name some people that the world considers to have "made it"—people who are successful, powerful, to be envied, or to be held up as role models. Discuss what they have done to earn this admiration. Give students several magazines and newspapers, and ask them to turn their thoughts into a group collage on the "Happy are…" poster board you prepared. Students should put pictures of the people they have talked about or any others that they think fall into the category of "successful (or happy) in the eyes of the world." Students may also use markers to add words or slogans to the collage.

When they've finished, challenge students to use the collage to help them complete this sentence: "The world says you've made it if…"

Ask: • **How strong are these messages? Are other routes to happiness and success promoted in society?**

Put the "Blessed are…" poster in front of the words "Happy are…" Say: **Jesus had something very different to say. He used the words "Blessed are…" when he** talked about the people who would be considered to be happy and to have "made it" in his kingdom.

Ask students to close their eyes and listen to these words of Jesus, then read Matthew 5:1-12 aloud.

Ask: • **Which of Jesus' statements seems most surprising to you?**

• **Which provides the biggest contrast with what the world says?**

• **How can you decide which of these messages is right? What would you want to know about the speaker of these words and the way the speaker lives his life before you chose who you were going to believe?**

• **Which message gives you more hope—the world's definition of happiness or Jesus' definition of blessedness? Why?**

Say: **Everybody wants to be happy and successful, but most people are looking in the wrong places and pursuing the wrong things. At the start of his ministry, Jesus took time to set out his vision of the kingdom of God, which is completely different from the way the world sees things—in fact it is upside down. Those who are blessed are not the wealthy or proud or successful, but the poor in spirit, the oppressed, and the persecuted.**

Finish by asking students to make themselves comfortable and close their eyes. Read the Beatitudes one more time, slowly. Leave students with this challenge: **Whose words are you going to believe and live by—Jesus' or the world's?**

small-group discussion 1

Discuss these questions in your small group:

· What are your dreams for the future? Where do you see yourself in ten years? What would you have liked to have achieved?

· What do you expect will bring you happiness and success?

· Is Jesus being realistic in the Beatitudes? Won't you just get trampled on if you try to live like this? Explain.

· How would you persuade someone that there is truth in Jesus' message?

teaching session 2: surprising blessings

Give everyone a couple of slips of paper. Ask students to write down some surprising facts about themselves that no one else will know. They could think of things they have done that seem out of character or dreams that they have for the future that will surprise others. For example, perhaps someone once dyed his or her hair bright red, or perhaps someone else has a secret desire to go parachuting. Give everyone the same kind of pen and get them to disguise their writing to make it more difficult. Fold all the slips and put them in a bowl. Students should each take a turn drawing out a slip and guessing who wrote it. Whether or not the guess is correct, the next student gets to draw a slip and take a guess.

After students have attempted to guess all of the surprises, ask: • **Has anything that you learned tonight changed your view of any of your friends? Explain.**

• **Was there anybody that you know so well that his or her surprises weren't actually surprising?**

Say: **As we saw yesterday, Jesus announced that in his kingdom surprising people would be blessed. Today we are going to explore some of those statements and see that actually they make a lot of sense.**

Have students form groups of two or three, and give each group one of the eight index cards you prepared containing Beatitudes and Bible stories. If you have less than eight groups, choose the Beatitudes that you think are most appropriate for your teenagers. Groups should each read the assigned Bible passage and discuss what the Beatitude on the card means. Invite students to use dictionaries for more insight into the meaning of their Beatitudes.

Have groups each draw a picture, write a story or poem, or create a piece of art showing a Christian who demonstrates this Beatitude today. They should explore how being like this can bring blessing, in spite of the fact that it is different from what the world says.

for younger teenagers

Just use some of the better-known stories from the index cards, such as Mary and Martha, Zacchaeus, or Paul and Silas, for younger students. Ask them to act out the Bible story first, showing how Jesus brought blessing to those people. Then prompt them to think of a modern-day equivalent to the story and act that out.

Prompt the groups to show their creations to one another, then ask: • **How difficult was it to think of examples of the Beatitudes in modern life?**

• **What is your reaction to seeing these pieces of art? Does it help you understand what Jesus was talking about? Explain.**

• **What questions do you still have about the Beatitudes?**

Finish this session by giving students an opportunity to think about whether they see themselves reflected in the Beatitudes. Say: **Some of the Beatitudes talk about how** someone might be feeling—poor in spirit, mourning, meek; some talk about what action people might take—showing mercy, making peace; and the last one is about what others might do to you—persecuting. **None of these are particularly easy or enjoyable, but Jesus says that they will bring blessing.**

Give students some time to reflect on which of the Beatitudes resonates with them. Conclude by asking them to write letters to God telling him how they feel and asking him to sustain them and bless them.

teaching session 3: secret agents

Split the students into three different groups and say: **Imagine you have been ship-wrecked on a desert island. There's plenty of food and building materials, so you will be able to survive. You know help is on the way, but it may take a few weeks for someone to get to you. In the meantime, you need to get along with everyone else in your group! Think about what kind of community you want to live in on the island. How do you expect people to treat each other? How will you share the work? What rules will you have?**

Give each group some time to discuss this, and ask them to write an "Island Charter," setting out their plans for their community. (You could provide the groups with tropical drinks and exotic fruits to eat to set the mood!)

Invite the groups to share their charters with the large group and explain why they chose various rules. Ask: • **How easy or difficult was it to write the charter?**

• **Were there things that you disagreed on in the group?**

• **Where did your ideas come from about what you should include?**

• **How different is your island charter from the way you live your life?**

• **What did you think of one another's charters? Are there any that you think won't work? Why?**

Say: **You have just decided how you will run your own micro-kingdoms—places where you are in charge and can make up the rules. Jesus talked a lot about the kingdom of God, but not as a separate escapist place, removed from our lives. He talked about the kingdom coming here on earth—every place that God's rule and reign is recognized and followed.**

Ask: • **Who knows the Lord's Prayer? Who can recite it?**

Invite a student to read Matthew 6:9-15. Say: **Every time this prayer is prayed, we pray for God's kingdom to come, but what exactly does that mean? You are about to investigate and find out!**

Have students form nine groups (a group can be as small as one person), and hand out a jigsaw puzzle poster piece to each group. They should read the passage and think about

leader tip

Need game ideas? Check out the game book suggestions on page 7!

leader tip

Students might be interested to know that the Gospel of Matthew talks about the kingdom of heaven and the Gospels of Mark and Luke talk about the kingdom of God. Matthew was writing mainly for Jewish readers. To a devout Jew, the word God was far too sacred to be used lightly or frequently, so Matthew talks about the kingdom of heaven. Mark and Luke prefer to use kingdom of God because it would have been easier for non-Jews to understand. The two expressions represent exactly the same idea.

what it tells them about the kingdom of God. Does it answer any of these questions: *What* is it? *Where* is it? *Who* is it for? *When* is it? *Why* is it important? *How* do people get into it?

When they've finished discussing their Scripture passages, groups should use art supplies to decorate their puzzle pieces to communicate what they have discovered. They can draw pictures, write words, or paint symbols.

Invite each group to share some feedback on the Scripture they read, then put the jigsaw pieces together to create a colorful, rich picture of the kingdom.

Ask: • **What is the most surprising thing you have discovered about the kingdom?**

• **How would you describe the kingdom of God to a ten-year-old child? Can you do it in one sentence, beginning "The kingdom of God is…"?**

Ask students to consider their place in the kingdom. God asks us to be his "secret agents" of the kingdom, spreading the good news of the kingdom wherever we can, by what we say and what we do. Give each student a small photo of themselves. (You will need to bring these from home, or have an instant-print camera, or digital camera, computer, and printer with you.) Ask the students to stick their photos on the jigsaw puzzle in the section that most resonates with their experience at the moment—maybe they are spreading the kingdom like the woman spreading the yeast through the dough or are prepared to make sacrifices for the kingdom like the merchant who bought the pearl. Conclude with a time of prayer.

---

small-group discussion 2

Discuss these questions in your small group:

· Is spreading the kingdom something that God does or something that we do, or both? Explain.

· How does society need to change to be more like the kingdom?

· How does each of us need to change to reflect the values of the kingdom?

---

teaching session 4: mission impossible?

Play the *Mission: Impossible* segment which shows Jim Phelps receiving his mission. Begin the clip at approximately 0:04:05 when Jim Phelps is offered a movie, and end the clip at approximately 0:06:15 when the tape self-destructs.

Say: **I have a mission to give you today that is more daring, more demanding, and more rewarding than any movie can portray. Are you going to accept it?**

Read Matthew 5:13-16. Say: **In these few verses, Jesus gives a mission to his** followers—to us. Being salt and light doesn't sound very dramatic, but if we rise to the challenge, this has the power to change the world.

Have two large pieces of poster board set out on the floor. In the middle of one, put a bowl of salt. Place a flashlight in the middle of the other. On the board surrounding the salt, students should write down all the different uses of salt that they can think of. On the board surrounding the light, students should write down as many different kinds of lights they can think of, and what those lights are used for. Allow plenty of time for students to come up with lots of examples.

When they've finished, ask: • **What do these uses of salt tell you about your role as a Christian in the world?**

• **Are there any uses of salt that don't seem to fit with being an agent of God's kingdom?**

On a flip chart, write "Our Mission" at the top. List the different tasks students named during the discussion about salt.

Now do a similar activity with the light poster. Ask: • **What do these different types of light tell us about who we should be as Christians?**

• **What do the different things that light is used for tell us about what we should do?**

List these under the "Our Mission" title.

Have students form pairs or trios, and pass out the index cards you prepared which contain scenarios the students are likely to encounter at school, church, or home. Ask each group to pick one of the cards and role-play the situation in front of the group, with one teenager portraying a Christian who is on a mission to be salt and light.

Finish the session with a worship experience, giving students an opportunity to decide whether they will accept this mission from Jesus—to be salt and light and to live out the values of the Beatitudes. Set up a large candle in the middle of the room, with some small candles next to it. Have some salty snacks available, such as salted nuts or pretzels. Make the room as dark as you can, and have students sit in a circle. Say: **Jesus gives you a role in helping to bring in his kingdom. Will you accept it?**

Light the large candle. Students who want to be light to the world should each take one of the small candles and light it, setting it down next to the large candle. Allow some time for people to do this. Point out that where there was one flame, there now are many. Next, invite the students to taste the salty foods and reflect on whether they will be salt in the world.

Conclude with a time of prayer, inviting students to each pray about one thing they will apply to their lives when they return home from the weekend.

leader tip

Bring all the different pieces of work done over the weekend into this session, and display them on the wall so students have a reminder of the many different things they have looked at and discussed.

STUDENT QUIET TIME 1: EXPECTATIONS

Think back on your journey with Christ—on how your life has been since you came to know Jesus. One way to help you remember is to think about each year since you became a Christian. What happened in that year? No doubt there were good experiences and bad. What were some of your mountaintop experiences when everything went well? How about valley experiences when it all went wrong? Which periods of your life were in sunshine (good feelings) and which in shadows (bad feelings)? Write them down here:

Mountains:

Valleys:

Sunshine:

Shadows:

God has been with you through all those experiences, whether you have been aware of him or not. Read Matthew 7:24-27. Being in the kingdom is no guarantee of an easy life. There *will* be storms—what matters is where your foundations are so that *when* the storms come you are not washed away. Tell God how you feel about this. What foundations have you built your life on?

Student Quiet Time 2:

Don't Worry!

(Instructions: Get a piece of string from your youth leader before you begin this quiet time.)

Worry— we all do it. Worry is not just being concerned about something—worry is returning to the same subject again and again, examining all the "What ifs?" Worry is like a CD track playing over and over in your mind. Worry paralyzes us and stops us enjoying the moment. So why do we do it?

Read Matthew 6:25-33.

■ What questions does Jesus ask in this passage? How would you answer them?

■ What reasons does Jesus give not to worry?

■ What things do you tend to worry about? Write down all your worries here. Tie a loose knot in your piece of string for each of your worries.

■ Worry leaves us in knots without sorting anything out. Look at each of your worries. How can you seek God's kingdom in these areas? Is there any action you can take instead of worrying?

■ Pray, asking God to help you not to worry, but to trust him. As you do so, undo the knots in your string and receive God's peace.

master supply list

In addition to basic retreat supplies such as food, games, Bibles, pens, pencils, paper, and worship music, you'll also need the following supplies:

- ❑ *Remember the Titans* video (or DVD)
- ❑ VCR (or DVD player)
- ❑ TV
- ❑ apple
- ❑ onion
- ❑ resealable plastic bag
- ❑ chalkboard and chalk (or dry-erase board and dry-erase markers)
- ❑ sidewalk chalk
- ❑ 1 photocopy of "Small-Group Discussion 1" box (p. 58) for each small group
- ❑ 1 photocopy of "Student Quiet Time 1: Shine" (p. 64) for each student
- ❑ rolls of butcher paper
- ❑ markers
- ❑ paints and paintbrushes
- ❑ several pieces of poster board
- ❑ 1 empty 2-liter plastic bottle for each small group
- ❑ 1 photocopy of "Small-Group Discussion 2" box (p. 61) for each small group
- ❑ 1 candle for each student
- ❑ matches
- ❑ 1 photocopy of "Student Quiet Time 2: The Least of These" (p. 65) for each student
- ❑ 1 shoe box for each student
- ❑ 1 lump of modeling clay or modeling dough for each student
- ❑ optional: a World War II book featuring pictures of the Holocaust, or a World War II documentary video
- ❑ optional: a large piece of junk such as a totaled car
- ❑ optional: spray paint
- ❑ optional: sledgehammer

leadership under construction

retreat focus: Students will study the leadership qualities of Nehemiah and will be challenged to follow his example in their own lives.

retreat motto: Christlike leaders follow Christ's lead.

theme verse: "Don't let anyone look down on you because you are young, but set an example for the believers in speech, in life, in love, in faith and in purity" (1 Timothy 4:12).

preparation

Before the retreat, gather all of the necessary supplies and make all of the photocopies recommended in the Master Supply List.

For Teaching Session 1, cue up *Remember the Titans* by setting the VCR counter at 0:00:00 when the studio logo appears before the movie starts. The segment you'll show starts at approximately 0:27:00 when the football practice scene begins. A few days before the retreat, place an apple in a resealable plastic bag with a chopped up onion. Keep the sealed bag in a refrigerator until Teaching Session 1, then rinse off the apple and throw the onion away. You'll also need to prepare the chalkboard (or dry-erase board) by creating a column on the left half of the board. Write the following titles in the column: Fossil Fuel Control Operator, Sanitation Artist, Merchandise Display Coordinator, Officer of Office Enhancement, Photo Efficiency Expert, Master of Foreign-Made Cutleries, Cured Meats Entrepreneur, and Vegetation Specialist. On the right half of the board, write these titles in a column: Hot Dog Vendor, One-Hour Photo Lab Guy, Ginsu Knife Salesman, Lawn Dude, Gas Station Attendant, Trash Man, Stock Boy, Secretary. Write "What's in a Name" at the top of the board.

> ### leader tip
>
> Avoid the embarrassment of showing the wrong scene—preview movie clips before using them!

For Teaching Session 3, use art supplies to create several posters and banners with inspirational messages on them such as "Way to go!" "Great job!" or "You're the best!"

For Teaching Session 4, put a piece of paper and a pencil inside each of the shoe boxes you've collected.

Make sure students are divided into small groups (for more information on this, see p. 7), and take some time to study the book of Nehemiah on your own.

worship idea

For your theme song for the weekend, use "Set Me on Fire" from the two-CD set *I Could Sing of Your Love Forever*. For information on ordering student lyrics books, a song leader book, and the CDs, call Group at 1-800-447-1070.

suggested schedule

2-Night Retreat

Day	Time	Activity	Supplies
Friday	6:00-7:00 p.m.	Games	
	7:00-8:00 p.m.	Teaching Session 1: What's in a Name?	Bibles, *Remember the Titans* video, TV, VCR, apple, onion, plastic bag, chalkboard, chalk
	8:00-9:30 p.m.	Free Time or Games	
	9:30-10:00 p.m.	Small-Group Discussion 1	Sidewalk chalk, photocopies of "Small-Group Discussion 1" box (p. 58) Optional: large sheets of butcher paper, markers
	10:00-10:30 p.m.	Snacks	
	11:00 p.m.	Lights Out	
Saturday	7:30-8:00 a.m.	Student Quiet Time 1: Shine	Bibles, photocopies of "Student Quiet Time 1: Shine" (p. 64), pens or pencils
	8:00-9:00 a.m.	Breakfast	
	9:00-10:00 a.m.	Teaching Session 2: Building Begins	Bibles, butcher paper, pens, markers Optional: WWII pictures or video clips, TV, VCR, totaled car, spray paint, sledgehammer
	10:00-11:30 a.m.	Games or Group Activities	
	11:30 a.m.-12:30 p.m.	Lunch	
	12:30-5:30 p.m.	Free Time or Group Activities	
	5:30-6:30 p.m.	Dinner	
	6:30-7:45 p.m.	Games	
	7:45-8:45 p.m.	Teaching Session 3: Building Up!	Bibles, posters and banners
	8:45-9:30 p.m.	Small-Group Discussion 2	Photocopies of "Small-Group Discussion 2" box (p. 61), empty bottles
	9:30-10:00 p.m.	Worship Session: Fire Power	Candles, matches
	10:00-10:30 p.m.	Snacks	
	11:00 p.m.	Lights Out	
Sunday	7:30-8:00 a.m.	Student Quiet Time 2: The Least of These	Bibles, photocopies of "Student Quiet Time 2: The Least of These" (p. 65), pencils or pens
	8:00-9:00 a.m.	Breakfast	
	9:00-10:00 a.m.	Teaching Session 4: A Lasting Impression	Bibles, shoe boxes, paper, pencils, modeling clay or modeling dough
	10:00 a.m.-noon	Games or Group Activities	

Day	Time	Activity	Supplies
Friday	6:00-7:30 p.m.	Games	
	7:30-8:30 p.m.	Teaching Session 2: Building Begins	Bibles, butcher paper, pens, markers Optional: totaled car, spray paint, sledgehammer, WWII pictures or video clips, TV, VCR
	8:30-9:00 p.m.	Small-Group Discussion 1	Photocopies of "Small-Group Discussion 1" box (p. 58), sidewalk chalk Optional: large sheets of butcher paper, markers
	9:00-9:30 p.m.	Worship Session: Fire Power	Candles, matches
	9:30-10:00 p.m.	Snacks	
	10:00-10:30 p.m.	Student Quiet Time 1: Shine	Bibles, photocopies of "Student Quiet Time 1: Shine" (p. 64), pencils or pens
	11:00 p.m.	Lights Out	
Saturday	7:30-8:00 a.m.	Student Quiet Time 2: The Least of These	Bibles, photocopies of "Student Quiet Time 2: The Least of These" (p. 65), pencils or pens
	8:00-9:00 a.m.	Breakfast	
	9:00-10:00 a.m.	Teaching Session 3: Building Up!	Bibles, posters and banners
	10:00-10:45 a.m.	Small-Group Discussion 2	Photocopies of "Small-Group Discussion 2" box (p. 61), empty bottles
	10:45 a.m.-noon	Games or Group Activities	

teaching session 1: what's in a name?

Before the session, select twelve students to participate in an activity. (For smaller groups, choose just four or five students.) Appoint one student to be the leader, and instruct the others that during the activity they will silently copy the leader's motions, movements, expressions, and gestures.

They should try to be inconspicuous about it, since everyone in the crowd will be trying to pick out which one of the dozen is the leader. Arrange the twelve in the front of the room in a semicircle so that they can clearly see one another, and ask remaining teenagers to try to guess who is leading and who is following.

Ask: • **What was challenging about this activity?**

• **How did you feel as you tried to determine who the leader was?**

• **How did you determine who the leader was?**

• **How do you determine who leaders are in real life?**

Display the chalkboard you prepared, and ask volunteers to take turns matching up the fancy names with their actual jobs by drawing lines from one to the other. When they've finished, review the following correct matches: Hot Dog Vendor and Cured Meats Entrepreneur, One-Hour Photo Lab Guy and Photo Efficiency Expert, Ginsu Knife Salesman with Master of Foreign-Made Cutleries, Lawn Dude and Vegetation Specialist,

leader tip

For an extra challenge, appoint three leaders, and have those remaining in the dozen follow any of the three. Those participating in the crowd should try and pick out which three they believe are leading the group.

Gas Station Attendant and Fossil Fuel Control Operator, Trash Man and Sanitation Artist, Stock Boy and Merchandise Display Coordinator, and Secretary with Officer of Office Enhancement.

Say: **Fancy titles don't really fool anyone. We are known by who we are and what we do, not by what we're called. In the same way, leadership is not just a title or position—it's about character. A leader, very simply put, is one who leads. If people aren't following, you aren't leading. A true leader inspires and influences in either positive or negative ways.**

Slice up the apple you have prepared, and ask a volunteer to taste it. Ask him or her to describe to the group how the apple tastes. (The apple will taste a little like onion.)

Say: **This apple was stored with an onion and absorbed much of the onion's flavor. A leader influences others in the same way—others in the group absorb the attitudes and characteristics of that person.**

Show a movie clip from *Remember the Titans*. Begin at approximately 0:27:00 when the team begins their scrimmage at practice. End the clip at approximately 0:30:45 when Julius tells Gerry, "Attitude reflect leadership, captain."

Ask a volunteer to read 1 Timothy 4:12 aloud. Say: **Whether or not we have been appointed to a specific leadership position, as a Christian each of us has the responsibility of leading others closer to God with our words and actions.**

Ask students to brainstorm specific ways to exhibit their faith in each of the elements listed in the verse—speech, life, love, faith, and purity.

Ask: • **Describe someone you know who leads by example, not necessarily because it is his or her position.**

• **What character traits do you think are the most important in a leader?**

Say: **In upcoming sessions, we'll be looking at the life of Nehemiah, an ordinary man who did something extraordinary.**

Encourage teenagers to look at the book of Nehemiah in their free time before meeting together again.

leader tip

You may want to begin each teaching session with five to ten minutes of singing. In addition to the suggested theme song, select other praise and worship songs that will complement the theme of the weekend.

small-group discussion 1

(Instructions: Get a piece of chalk from your youth leader before you begin this discussion. If your retreat area doesn't have cement sidewalks or parking lots, ask your youth leader for markers and a piece of butcher paper.)

Go outside and trace the silhouette of one of your group members on the cement. After you've completed the body outline, take turns writing down important leadership qualities by different body parts that can represent those qualities. For example, someone could write "Reaches out to hurting people" by the hand or "Sees needs" by the eyes. When you've finished, discuss these questions in your small group:

- *Of the qualities we've listed, which are the most important?*

- *Which are the hardest to live out?*

- *Think of some current leaders—at school, in government, or in church. How well do they live out these characteristics?*

- *How does your own example of leadership compare to the traits we've discussed?*

teaching session 2: building begins

Cover an inside wall in a well-ventilated area of your meeting space with butcher paper, and supply markers and pens (and spray paint if you're brave). Give students ten minutes to "vandalize" the wall, writing their names and messages onto the paper.

ACTION

for extra **impact**

For a true adventure, find something on a larger scale that students may "vandalize" (with permission, of course)—by carving their names in a picnic table, for example, or signing their names with markers on a shed that will soon be repainted. You could even consider having a totaled car towed from a junkyard and allowing students to paint the outside or take whacks at it with a mallet or sledgehammer!

for younger teenagers

For middle school and junior high students, make sure you have ample supervision for this activity. You don't want the retreat center walls to actually be vandalized! Also make sure you give younger teenagers a clear idea of what is and is not acceptable grafitti—curse words, inappropriate pictures, or rude references to other students should not be tolerated.

Say: **Try to imagine what it would be like if someone vandalized your home, school, or church—someplace that was especially dear to you.**

Ask: • **What emotions would you feel?**

Explain that long ago the people of Israel had been forced to leave their homeland.

Those who survived returned years later to find Jerusalem totally trashed. The people felt completely disgraced.

Ask a volunteer to read Nehemiah 1:1-11 aloud, then say: **The Jews in Nehemiah's day didn't know where or how to begin the painful process of rebuilding their city and their lives. At the time they returned, Nehemiah was working as a cupbearer to a king in the city of Susa. When he heard about what had happened to Jerusalem and the heartache of his people, he wept. Then he prayed. Compassion and prayer make a powerful combination!**

Ask: • **Based on this limited information, how would you describe Nehemiah?**

• **How can a person's prayer life be a measure of the success of his or her leadership?**

Say: **Nehemiah was a man of compassion, prayer, and courage. The king couldn't help but notice that Nehemiah was down. When King Artaxerxes asked him about it, Nehemiah got up the courage to request a transfer. The king liked Nehemiah and supported his idea, so Nehemiah traveled to Jerusalem to help his people rebuild the city wall. The king took good care of Nehemiah, sending letters and soldiers to make his passage to Jerusalem an easy one. Finally they arrived, and in the middle of the night Nehemiah rode around the city wall, looking over the damage. He knew in his heart that God's plan was to rebuild the wall and the city, and the next morning he inspired his people to do it! People who had begun to feel devastated by their loss felt a hope and excitement they had long forgotten.**

Ask students to read Nehemiah 4 silently, paying extra attention to verses 6-10 and 21-23. After a few minutes have passed, ask students to use their Bibles to answer the following questions:

• **What sort of opposition did Nehemiah and the Jews face?**

• **How did they overcome these obstacles?**

Say: **Nehemiah brought out the best in his workers. One reason is that he was willing to work so hard himself. He was always on guard. He and his men worked around the clock.**

Ask: • **Why is it important for a leader to serve, doing even the most undesirable jobs alongside others?**

• **How was Nehemiah able to motivate his workers to work tirelessly, even risking their lives, for the project at hand?**

• **What quality do you most respect about Nehemiah?**

Challenge each student to answer the last question silently and consider ways to develop that quality in his or her own life.

for extra **impact**

To help students understand what this experience might have been like, talk about the Holocaust, reminding students how families were separated and left wondering if their loved ones were even still alive. After the war they sadly returned to their lives and slowly tried to rebuild them, knowing they would never be the same. To make the point, consider showing photos of concentration camp victims being liberated or appropriate video clips from a World War II documentary.

leader tip

Need game ideas? Check out the game book suggestions on page 7!

teaching session 3: building up!

Before the session, decorate the meeting area with the posters and banners of inspirational messages you prepared.

ACTION

To begin, ask teenagers to form groups of six to eight students, and ask each group to create a cheer to encourage others present in the crowd. If they need ideas to get them started, let them know the names of individuals who have done something outstanding during the weekend, such as picking up trash or helping with meals. They could cheer individuals who have a big event coming up in their lives, such as taking the ACT or applying for a summer job. Give the groups several minutes to develop their cheers, and then allow teams one by one to perform their routines for the others.

Share something about Nehemiah's character with your students. Explain that Nehemiah was an encourager. He cheered on the people as they rebuilt the wall of the city. When they would lose their courage or begin to give in to the criticism of their opposition, or when they just felt worn out from working day and night, he maintained a positive attitude, building them up, reassuring them, and leading them in prayer. Tell your students that the wall was completed in record time—fifty-two days! The surrounding nations were amazed, and they feared Israel because they were sure God was on Israel's side. Nehemiah gave the glory to God.

Ask a volunteer to read Nehemiah 5:14-18 aloud, then say: **Nehemiah really cared about the people he was placed in charge of. He didn't charge them the usual taxes that would pay his salary. Imagine how unusual it would be if a president or member of Congress turned down his or her salary! Nehemiah went even further. Every single day, he would feed over 150 people. That took an enormous amount of food. He asked for nothing in return because he understood the demands already on his people.**

Challenge your students to try to think of modern examples of leaders who have made sacrifices similar to Nehemiah's.

Ask a volunteer to read Nehemiah 6:1-9. Invite several students to summarize the passage. Make sure all of the students understand that Nehemiah's life was endangered, yet he was wise and brave and followed God's leading. He was able to do this because he was in constant communication with God, praying to him about every event and decision. Nehemiah was encouraging, self-sacrificing, and courageous, but the quality that best equipped him for leadership was his desire to draw his people closer to the Lord.

Ask someone to read Nehemiah 8:1-3 and 8:9-10. Say: **Nehemiah gave all the credit to God. But God used him in a really special way to almost single-handedly transform a nation from despair to joy.**

Ask: • **What qualities made Nehemiah an excellent leader?**

• **What role did encouragement play in the speedy completion of the city wall?**

• **How did Nehemiah show the people the importance of prayer?**

Prompt your students to spend some time in prayer, like Nehemiah, asking God for the courage and wisdom to lead others wisely and sacrificially.

small-group discussion 2

(Instructions: Get one empty bottle from your youth leader before you begin this discussion.)

Play a new version of "Spin the Bottle" with your group by sitting in the circle and placing the bottle in the middle on its side. Take turns spinning the bottle. Share an encouraging compliment with whoever the mouth of the bottle is pointing toward when it stops spinning. After everyone has been complimented at least once, discuss these questions in your small group:

· How might you learn to compliment your peers in a meaningful way, not just flatter them?

· How does encouragement bring out the best in people?

· What can you do to draw your friends and peers closer to God?

worship session: fire power

Distribute a candle to each student and have them gather around an outdoor campfire. Invite adult leaders to help you light the students' candles. Explain to the teenagers how fire can be used for good or for destruction. We use it to cook food, kill germs, shape metal—but within moments, a fire that's not carefully harnessed can wipe out a forest, destroy a home, and even kill people or animals. Ask students to contribute some examples of ways that fire is used for good. Next, ask them to brainstorm some of the dangers of fire.

Ask: **• How can leaders use their influence for good? Give examples.**

• How can leaders use their influence in negative or hurtful ways? Give examples.

Say: **The importance of your influence is greater than you can ever imagine. Like this flame, your influence can be beneficial or destructive.**

Ask students to silently think of times their influence as leaders has hurt others, and prompt them to repent of those actions and accept God's forgiveness. Close with a time of silent prayer, encouraging students to pray with their eyes open, watching the flame of their candles. Encourage them to dedicate their leadership opportunities to God and to ask for his guidance in how they affect others' lives.

teaching session 4: a lasting impression

Distribute the shoe boxes you prepared as students assemble for the final session. Explain that a time capsule is a container that is filled with small items characterizing a particular time period. The capsules are buried, and when they are discovered they're like nuggets of history, shedding light on the lives of people who lived some time ago.

Ask teenagers to think about the qualities or acts they would like to be remembered for as leaders, and what small items might symbolize those things. Students should imagine the box is a time capsule and use the paper to write down the items they would fill the box with if the box represented their time on earth. They might choose pre-existing facts or characteristics about themselves, or they might want to think in terms of what they would like to become. For instance, a student with ambitions of becoming a medical missionary might write down things like: Bible, stethoscope, and map. A sports-minded student might write down things like an Olympic gold medal, a stopwatch, and a small American flag. Students should feel free to write down as many items as they think would fit in the box. Give teenagers an opportunity to share what they have written with the group. Afterward, ask several volunteers to read Nehemiah 5:19; 13:14; 13:22; and 13:31 aloud.

Say: **Nehemiah didn't care who got the credit for the exciting things that were happening in the city, and he gave God all the glory. But still, he wanted God to remember that he had invested his heart in the lives of the Jewish people. Nehemiah had already witnessed that construction isn't permanent. But God showed him that goodness can't be destroyed.**

Give each student a lump of clay, and direct them on how to mold it, but don't tell them what they are making. Choose something in advance—a duck or a frog, for example, and give vague instructions such as, "Form the clay into a ball. Make a lump at one end with a skinny piece coming out of it. Shape a rounded knob on top of the fat end of the lump…" Afterward, tell them what they've been making, and allow them to show off their masterpieces.

Invite several students to rate their own sculptures on a scale of 1 to 5, 1 being "unidentifiable blob of clay" and 5 being "a perfect representation."

After several students have shared their ratings, ask: • **How did you feel as you shaped your clay into a final product?**

• **How is leading others like creating a sculpture?**

• **What are some things leaders sometimes do that can misshape others' lives?**

• **How can leaders affect others' lives in a positive way, helping to shape them into masterpieces?**

Say: **As leaders, you have the challenging responsibility of shaping lives. Your duties extend beyond organizing events, building programs, or planning activities.**

Those things won't last. But the goodness you show to others, as you help mold their lives into what God intends them to be, will never be forgotten.

Ask: • **What are some ways you can make a lasting difference in the lives of your peers?**

• **If you could hear your peers talking about you, what would you hope to hear them say?**

• **How do you hope to be remembered?**

Ask students to debrief in small groups of three or four. Challenge teenagers to pray together, committing to greater involvement and influence in the lives of their peers.

Close with a time of prayer for your students, asking God for a special blessing on the young people he has entrusted with such important responsibilities.

Student Quiet Time 1: Shine

This unwelcome visitor is present at nearly every major event in life—prom, graduation, the big first date, even the wedding day. It is the untimely break out, the planet-sized zit that takes on a life of its own. It refuses to be covered or hidden. Makeup can't mask it. Even a Band-Aid can't make it disappear. It shines through like a beacon, telling everyone of its presence at just a glance. There are things about our outsides that we can't hide very well, and things inside of us that can't be hidden either.

A person can't disguise his or her character—or lack of it. First impressions may fool people for a while, but eventually people come to know us for who we are and what we do—even in secret—good or bad.

The single best thing you can do for the peers you lead is to fall in love with Jesus.

Read Matthew 5:13-16.

• How do I want to be viewed by my peers?

• What behaviors in my life would I not want others to copy?

• As a leader, how can my character influence others for good or for evil?

Student Quiet Time 2:

The Least of These

Use your fingers to count out ten friends or acquaintances in your life that you like—you have fun with them and enjoy hanging out together. Let each finger represent a person. Why do you like these people? What makes you gravitate toward them?

Now use your fingers to count out ten other people—people you don't notice much, don't talk to, or don't like very much. Think of ten specific people who may be social outcasts or who are different from you. Be honest—you don't really talk to them. You definitely don't naturally gravitate toward them…in fact some of them actually repel you. Let each finger represent one specific person.

Can you love these people? Can you serve them?

As a leader, Jesus loved and served forgotten, grungy people. In fact, for his dozen apprentices he handpicked a variety of outcasts—a despised tax collector; simple, uneducated fishermen; and even a greedy traitor. He entrusted them with wisdom. He inspired them with a dream. He served them with love.

And they changed the world forever.

Read Mark 3:13-15.

• Who am I reaching out to who doesn't really fit into my circle of friends?

• How am I mentoring forgotten peers and shaping them for greater service?

• As a leader, how can I go about changing lives for the better?

loving the "unlovely"

retreat focus: Students will study the book of Jonah and will be challenged to live out its message about God's love for *all* people—even those who are hard to love.

retreat motto: Beauty is only skin deep—but ugly goes to the bone.

theme verse: "But God demonstrates his own love for us in this: While we were still sinners, Christ died for us" (Romans 5:8).

preparation

Before the retreat, gather all of the necessary supplies and make all of the photocopies recommended in the Master Supply List.

For Teaching Session 1, cue up *Snow White and the Seven Dwarfs* by setting the VCR counter to 0:00:00 when the studio logo appears before the movie starts. The segment you'll show starts at approximately 0:01:35 when the storybook opens.

Make sure students are divided into small groups (for more information on this, see p. 7), and take some time to study the book of Jonah on your own.

leader tip

Avoid the embarrassment of showing the wrong scene—preview movie clips before using them!

worship idea

For your theme song for the weekend, use "You Are Merciful to Me" from the two-CD set *I Could Sing of Your Love Forever*. For information on ordering student lyrics books, a song leader book, and the CDs, call Group at 1-800-447-1070.

master supply list

In addition to basic retreat supplies such as food, games, Bibles, pens, pencils, paper, and worship music, you'll also need the following supplies:

❏ *Snow White and the Seven Dwarfs* video (or DVD)
❏ VCR (or DVD player)
❏ TV
❏ 1 photocopy of "Small-Group Discussion 1" box (p. 70) for each small group
❏ 1 photocopy of "Student Quiet Time 1: Who Are the Unlovely?" (p. 75) for each student
❏ 1 photocopy of "Jonah Evaluation" handout (p. 77) for each pair of students
❏ 1 photocopy of "Small-Group Discussion 2" box (p. 72) for each small group
❏ 1 photocopy of "Student Quiet Time 2: You, Un-plugged" (p. 76) for each student
❏ chair
❏ hand mirror
❏ piece of clear glass (without sharp edges)

suggested schedule

2-Night Retreat

Day	Time	Activity	Supplies
Friday	6:00-7:00 p.m.	Games	
	7:00-8:00 p.m.	Teaching Session 1: Inside vs. Outside	*Snow White and the Seven Dwarfs* video, VCR, TV, paper, pencils
	8:00-9:30 p.m	Free Time or Games	
	9:30-10:00 p.m.	Small-Group Discussion 1	Photocopies of "Small-Group Discussion "1 box (p. 70)
	10:00-10:30 p.m.	Snacks	
	11:00 p.m.	Lights Out	
Saturday	7:30-8:00 a.m.	Student Quiet Time 1: Who Are the Unlovely?	Bibles, photocopies of "Student Quiet Time 1: Who Are the Unlovely?" (p. 75), pencils or pens
	8:00-9:00 a.m.	Breakfast	
	9:00-10:00 a.m.	Teaching Session 2: Operation Rescue Nineveh	Bibles, photocopies of "Jonah Evaluation" handout (p. 77), pencils or pens
	10:00-10:30 a.m.	Free Time	
	10:30 a.m.-noon	Games or Group Activities	
	noon-1:00 p.m.	Lunch	
	1:00-3:00 p.m.	Free Time	
	3:00-4:00 p.m.	Teaching Session 3: Told You So	Bibles
	4:00-5:00 p.m.	Free Time	
	5:00-6:00 p.m.	Dinner	
	6:00-9:30 p.m.	Games or Group Activities	
	9:30-10:00 p.m.	Small-Group Discussion 2	Photocopies of "Small-Group Discussion 2" box (p. 72)
	10:00-10:30 p.m.	Snacks	
	11:00 p.m.	Lights Out	
Sunday	7:30-8:00 a.m.	Student Quiet Time 2: You, Unplugged	Bibles, photocopies of "Student Quiet Time 2: You, Unplugged" (p. 76), pencils or pens
	8:00-9:00 a.m.	Breakfast	
	9:00-10:00 a.m.	Teaching Session 4: I Love Human-kind—It's People I Can't Stand	Bibles, empty chair
	10:00-11:00 a.m.	Worship Session: God's Eyes	Hand mirror, piece of clear glass
	11:00 a.m.-noon	Games or Group Activities	

Day	Time	Activity	Supplies
Friday	6:00-7:00 p.m.	Teaching Session 2: Operation Rescue Nineveh	Bibles, photocopies of "Jonah Evaluation" handout (p. 77), pencils or pens
	7:00-8:30 p.m.	Games	Bibles
	8:30-9:30 p.m.	Teaching Session 3: Told You So	Photocopies of "Small-Group Discussion 1" box (p. 70)
	9:30-10:00 p.m.	Snacks	
	10:00-10:30 p.m.	Small-Group Discussion 1	Bibles, photocopies of "Student Quiet Time 2: You, Unplugged" (p. 72), pens or pencils
	11:00 p.m.	Lights Out	
Saturday	7:30-8:00 a.m.	Student Quiet Time 2: You, Unplugged	Bibles, empty chair
	8:00-9:00 a.m.	Breakfast	
	9:00-10:00 a.m.	Games or Group Activities	
	10:00-11:00 a.m.	Teaching Session 4: I Love Human-kind—It's People I Can't Stand	Hand mirror, piece of clear glass
	11:00 a.m.-noon	Worship Session: God's Eyes	

teaching session 1: inside vs. outside

Have teenagers form same-sex trios, and distribute one piece of paper and one pencil (with an eraser) to each teenager.

Say: **Welcome to the first annual Assembly of Biological Sciences. As the most talented group of biotech scientists ever gathered in one place, you are the perfect group to do what has never been done before: to design your ideal spouses. In the next ten minutes you'll each sketch a picture of your ideal spouse. Draw in as much detail as you can, because your sketches will be given to a crack team of biotechnologists and plastic surgeons who'll use those sketches to create your ideal spouses.**

After ten minutes have passed, ask teenagers to use the sketches to introduce their future spouses to their trios, explaining what they drew and why those characteristics are so important in a perfect spouse. Then ask for several volunteers to introduce their perfect spouses to the larger group.

for younger teenagers

Middle schoolers may think having a spouse is so far distant in the future that it's hard to make the leap. Substitute the idea of drawing an ideal hero instead.

Say: **Clearly some of you have already given this matter a great deal of thought! But notice how much time we spent describing the physical attributes of our perfect spouses rather than their intellectual, spiritual, or emotional attributes.**

Prompt students to listen carefully as you give them two options from which to select. To explain option one, say: **Your future spouse is everything you've described**

leader tip

Avoid explosions among your dating couples by adding a caveat: The perfect mate must not resemble a person the artist is currently dating.

physically—and more. Stunning. Buff. Attractive beyond belief. And your future spouse *knows* it—and is accustomed to getting his or her way *because* of his or her physical perfection. None of your friends describes this person as particularly nice, or caring, or considerate—just beautiful and rich.

Now explain option two, stating: **Your future spouse is attractive, but hardly perfect. That's not a problem, because the person doesn't worry too much about his or her physical shortcomings. Your future mate is usually focused on others. This is a person who gets involved in good causes, loves God, and does well in school and at work. Your future spouse has a sense of humor and a capacity for compassion.**

Ask: • **Who would you pick as your future spouse?**

Ask for a show of hands for each option.

Say: **If we're honest, we'll admit that we have a tendency to treat others better if they're beautiful, rich, famous, or talented. It's human nature.**

Fortunately, it's not *God's* nature. God isn't dazzled by exteriors. He values *interiors*. Not how we look, but who we are. Not how well we advertise, but how well we deliver the goods. God sees us clearly in a world where we often don't see others or ourselves clearly at all. In God's view, even people we see as unlovely are lovable. And sometimes what appears beautiful and lovely on the outside isn't so lovely at all.

Show the *Snow White and the Seven Dwarfs* clip beginning at 0:01:35 when the storybook opens. Stop the tape when the counter reaches 0:03:10 when the witch asks, "Magic mirror on the wall, who is the fairest one of all?" (Ask a student to read the text aloud on the storybook as pages flip past.)

Ask teenagers to form trios and discuss:

• **If a magic mirror existed that showed all the lovely people in your town, would your picture appear? Why or why not?**

• **What makes a person lovely in the truest sense of the word?**

• **What sort of people would *not* make the "lovely" cut? Why?**

• **What if God was in charge of the mirror? Would there be people who were so unlovely that even *God* couldn't tolerate them?**

Say: **At this retreat we'll consider how to love unlovely people—those who don't look lovely, those who don't act lovely, those who others might consider unlovable. We'll consider how God views us, and we'll look at the issue through the eyes of the Patron Saint of Dismissing the Unlovely: the prophet, Jonah.**

leader tip

You may want to begin each teaching session with five to ten minutes of singing. In addition to the suggested theme song, select other praise and worship songs that will complement the theme of the weekend.

small-group discussion 1

Discuss these questions in your small group:

• Confession time: Who is the most beautiful (or handsome) person you've seen on television or in the movies? What makes the person beautiful? Defend your choice if others disagree.

• In your opinion, what makes someone unlovable?

• Imagine you've been given a pair of glasses that lets you see the world—and the people in it—exactly as God views things. What would you see during a typical day?

teaching session 2: operation rescue nineveh

Ask teenagers to form pairs with someone who wasn't in their previous trio and to read Jonah 1:1–3:10 together.

After students finish reading the passage, say: **Jonah was a prophet and a reasonably smart guy. So why would he respond to God's instructions to go to Nineveh by immediately sailing in the other direction? His behavior makes more sense when we know more about the city of Nineveh.**

Give teenagers some background information about Nineveh by explaining that it was a large city of at least 120,000 inhabitants. A wall more than seven miles long circled the city. And it sat in the worst possible place for a Jewish prophet to go on a short-term missionary trip: Assyria.

Let them know that the nation of Assyria was well-known for cruelty. In earlier years Israel had paid tribute to the Assyrian king Shalmaneser III. Jonah probably knew of the suffering Syria had endured as it repelled recent Assyrian attacks. From Jonah's perspective, he was on a mission that would surely get him killed—probably in a terrible way.

Challenge teenagers to consider what they would have done in Jonah's position. Would they be willing to walk into that city and threaten destruction if the city did not repent? Ask for a show of hands—students who *would* do it and then students who *wouldn't*. Ask for volunteers from each group to explain their rationale.

Distribute a photocopy of the "Jonah Evaluation" handout (p. 77) and a pencil or pen to each pair of teenagers. Invite the students to take a few minutes to fill out their "reports" about Jonah's performance, and then ask pairs to form foursomes and compare answers. Ask for a vote regarding whether to fire Jonah for performance failure. Explore the reasons behind kids' votes.

Say: **Jonah doesn't come off as a hero here. He's willing to let 120,000 people tank so he doesn't have to wade into the midst of a culture he despises. But God saw the Ninevites differently from how Jonah saw them. He still loved them enough to send a messenger to tell them how they could avoid the consequences of their evil lives. We serve a God who believes in second chances and midcourse corrections.**

It's easy to criticize Jonah because he's an easy target, but God also sends us into _our_ world to share his message of hope. And we, too, sometimes go in the opposite direction. We don't want to wade into a fallen culture. We don't want to risk having people misunderstand us or our motives. We're proud. We're scared. We fear criticism. In many ways we're like Jonah. Should God fire us or work with us to help us grow?

Encourage students to answer the question you've put to them as a group. Then ask teenagers to discuss the following:

• **Think about your town or school. Where is the place you'd least like God to send you to talk with people about repenting? Why?**

• **If someone filled out an evaluation form about you—like the one you've filled out about Jonah—how would you do?**

teaching session 3: told you so

Ask for three volunteers willing to read Bible verses aloud. Explain to the rest of your teenagers that they're now charter members of the All-Mime-No-Prop Cheap-Seats-Only Theater Company. Cast these roles for your first performance: Jonah, Vine, Worm, Shelter (2 teenagers), Ninevites, and a two-person Sound Effects Crew.

Place the Ninevites (as many teenagers as you wish, up to 120,000 total!) at the center of the stage, and have Jonah stand with them. Place the Shelter, Vine, Worm, and Sound Effects Crew on one side of the stage, and the Readers on the other side. Give each Reader a Bible. Explain to the actors that they are to mime the actions in the script as it is read. Let the Sound Effects Crew know that their job is to insert silly sound effects to go along with the action.

Begin the script by saying: **The city of Nineveh was mighty, the capital of the entire Assyrian Empire. The men of the city went about their jobs—some as carpenters or working in other trades, and some who were religious and government leaders. The women worked just as hard tending to children and caring for their homes. The Ninevites were much like us—busy, bustling, and distracted by the challenges of daily life. In this city of great learning, they knew a lot, but they didn't know that they were in great danger.**

That is, not until God sent Jonah to tell them that unless they repented and changed in forty days, the city would fall into the hands of one of Assyria's enemies.

leader tip

Need game ideas? Check out the game book suggestions on page 7!

So they repented. They fell down on their knees and asked for forgiveness. And Jonah saw that his simple message of hope had a huge impact.

Instruct your Readers to begin reading with Jonah 4:1, alternating verses until they've read through verse 11. Applaud your actors enthusiastically at the end of their performance.

Ask teenagers to form trios and then discuss:

• **In what ways did Jonah reveal that he, too, was unlovely?**

• **In what ways do you agree or disagree with Jonah's behavior?**

• **What did you discover about the character of God in this encounter with Jonah?**

Say: **The Ninevites weren't the *only* unlovely ones in this story. It's tough to love Jonah, too, when he's not at his best. But note what we learn about God: God is patient with Jonah. He acts with love for both the Ninevites, who repent of their sinful ways, and Jonah, who is slow to repent of his pride and stubbornness. God is willing to love the unlovely—even people like Jonah. Even people like us.**

small-group discussion 2

Discuss these questions in your small group:

· Think about your life: In what ways are you like Jonah? unlike Jonah?

· If you were God—and let's be thankful you aren't—how would you have handled the "Nineveh-is-evil" situation?

· If you were deputized as a "prophet" today and told to carry a message to your school next week, what message do you think it would be? What would happen if you walked the halls saying it?

teaching session 4: i love humankind—it's people i can't stand

Say: **Loving the unlovely demands more than an act of the will—it requires a God-inspired change of heart.**

Jonah didn't make it—at least not by the time the book about him ends. He's still sulking, still wanting the Ninevites to get what they deserve. He wants to see justice, not grace. And what God wants is to see Jonah's heart soften toward the people in Nineveh.

God is still in the heart-softening business.

Ask teenagers to form trios with people with whom they haven't yet teamed up, and place an empty chair in a prominent spot in the room where everyone can see it. If possible, dim the lights in the room except for a light that illuminates the chair.

Encourage your students to each picture someone they know sitting in the chair—someone they consider unlovely. Maybe it's a bully who takes advantage of them. Or it might be a teacher who dismisses their faith as nonsense and who treats them with disdain. Maybe it's someone who treats them like they're not even alive.

Say: **Take a moment to silently put that person in this chair.** (Pause.) **Look at the person closely. How do you feel when you're in the presence of this person?** (Pause.) **What is it about this person that makes him or her unlovely in your eyes?** (Pause.)

In your trios, without revealing the identity of the person you've placed in this chair, describe the person. Describe how you feel around him or her. Tell your partners why you've felt this person is unlovely.

Give students a few minutes for discussion.

Next prompt students to imagine that Jesus has entered the room. Say: **He smiles at the group and we smile back. Then he sees you in the crowd and gives you a nod. He's walking over to you. He gives you a hug, and then he turns to see what you thought you alone could see: that person in the chair. He knows who you've put there, who you consider unlovely. He looks at you again, and he's inviting you to see the person the way *he* sees him or her.**

Standing next to the chair, read the following passages aloud: Matthew 9:9-13 and Luke 19:1-10.

Have students discuss the following questions in their trios:

• **How does Jesus view the person you've placed in the chair? Why?**

• **How does Jesus expect you to view the person in the chair? What makes it difficult for you to see the person as Jesus sees the person?**

• **What's one thing you could do in the next week that would reflect Jesus' view of the person? Will you do it? Why or why not?**

After trios have had time to discuss the questions, form a large circle. Place the chair in the ring of teenagers as if it were a person. Have everyone hold hands, but don't have students on each side of the chair reach across it to hold hands.

Conclude with a prayer, asking God to help the students apply their commitments to their lives when they return home from the retreat.

worship session: god's eyes

Gather your teenagers in a circle on the floor (or several circles if you have more than thirty kids). Pass around a small mirror, and ask that each student briefly look into it and make eye contact with his or her reflection before passing the mirror along.

Say: **How we're seeing ourselves now is how most other people see us. They see our outsides. They notice our imperfections. They assume things about us because we do or don't wear contact lenses, or have braces, or have a certain skin color. They react to our age…to our clothing…to our accent… All they see is what's on the outside.**

Set the mirror aside as it reaches you, then pass around a piece of clear glass for students to look in as they did with the mirror.

Say: **God looks straight through our exteriors and sees our interior lives. He sees our hearts. He sees what we value. He knows our motivations. He sees who we are inside. God is not fooled or distracted by our exteriors. He knows us better than that—and he loves us anyway. He loves us enough to send his Son to die in our place on a cross, so we can be in a loving, restored relationship with him.**

And God loves the unlovely people in our lives just as much. Through his power, how can we do less? Let's seek to look at others the way God sees them— not the way everyone else sees them. Let's seek to see and value interiors, not exteriors.

Share a prayer and worship time honoring God for allowing unlovely people like us to be accepted as sons and daughters, full heirs in God's kingdom.

Student Quiet Time 1:
Who Are the Unlovely?

OK, so we're enlightened.

Accepting.

Tolerant of others.

That still doesn't mean we want just *anyone* as a locker partner.

Be honest. Nobody will see this journal page unless you choose to show it to someone. Who are the unlovely people on your list? People with AIDS? People who commit acts of terrorism? People of other races? People who oppress or abuse the innocent? People of other religions—or no religion at all? Who's there? And why?

If God sent you to their hangout, home address, or hospital ward, would you go? Why or why not? What would it cost you to make the effort?

Read John 3:16. How would those people look if you viewed them through Jesus' eyes?

Student Quiet Time 2: YOU, UNPLUGGED

Read Jonah 4:1-4.

Ah—the big question. The one that only God has the right to ask: Have you any right to be angry?

We get angry and consider people unlovely because they inconvenience us, consume a resource we think we deserve, get a break we don't get, or have the nerve to be different from us. But if God is patient and loving with those people, what gives us the right to be angry? Or jealous? Or superior? We're like Jonah. What have those unlovely people done to us that we haven't done to others—or to God?

If you want to love the unlovely, you must first admit that you, too, are unlovely apart from God's grace. The ground is level at the foot of the cross—you're no better than the next sinner who shows up to be forgiven. Then you must decide to let God's grace work in and through you and to share the grace you've received from God with others. After all, God didn't give you his love with the idea you'd hold it close to *your* heart alone. God intends for you to share it, too.

What unlovely things have you done that you need to confess to God? to others?

In what ways do anger, fear, or indifference block your willingness to share God's love with others? What would happen if you let go of what keeps you from loving the unlovely?

Apart from God's grace, we're all unlovely. Forgiven by God, you are lovely in God's eyes. Have you received God's forgiveness? How do you see yourself?

Jonah Evaluation

Operative: __Jonah__

Mission: **Carry message of hope to the 120,000 inhabitants of Nineveh.**

In thirty words or less, indicate actions Operative took to fulfill the mission:

_____

_____

_____

Describe Operative's attitude toward the mission:

_____

_____

_____

Describe Operative:

What does Operative appear to value?

_____

_____

_____

What are three words that describe Operative's character?

_____

_____

_____

What are Operative's strengths and weaknesses?

_____

_____

_____

Your recommendation about continuing to employ Operative:

Based on Operative's performance, would you recommend using Operative for another mission or firing Operative? Why?

_____

_____

_____

Your name[s]: _____

the nerve to serve

master supply list

In addition to basic retreat supplies such as food, games, Bibles, pens, pencils, paper, and worship music, you'll also need the following supplies:

- ❏ 1 cookie for each student
- ❏ 1 cup of juice for each student
- ❏ 4 aprons
- ❏ a selection of dictionaries, thesauruses, and concordances
- ❏ butcher paper
- ❏ markers
- ❏ 1 photocopy of "Small-Group Discussion 1" box (p. 81) for each small group
- ❏ 1 photocopy of "Student Quiet Time 1: My Feet?!" (p. 87) for each student
- ❏ 6 tennis balls
- ❏ tennis racket
- ❏ pitcher
- ❏ basin
- ❏ small table
- ❏ towel
- ❏ magazines, current newspapers, news printouts (from the Internet), flyers or newsletters from local charities
- ❏ glue sticks
- ❏ 1 index card for each student
- ❏ several pairs of scissors
- ❏ 1 photocopy of "Small-Group Discussion 2" box (p. 85) for each small group
- ❏ 1 photocopy of "Student Quiet Time 2: Feelin' Good" (p. 88) for each student
- ❏ garbage bags and cleaning supplies
- ❏ colored construction paper

retreat focus: Students will be inspired to serve others by taking a closer look at Jesus' own example of servanthood.

retreat motto: Serving others, serving God

theme verse: "Now that I, your Lord and Teacher, have washed your feet, you also should wash one another's feet" (John 13:14).

preparation

Before the retreat, gather all of the necessary supplies and make all of the photocopies recommended in the Master Supply List.

For Teaching Session 1, set up a table of juice and cookies, enough for one drink and one cookie for each student. You'll also need to tape a large sheet of butcher paper across one wall of your meeting area.

For Teaching Session 2, use a permanent marker to write one of the following Scripture references on each tennis ball: Luke 1:74; Romans 1:9; Romans 12:11-14; Ephesians 6:7; Colossians 3:23-24; 1 Peter 4:11.

For Teaching Session 4, identify several cleaning projects that can be done at your retreat location, and gather the appropriate cleaning supplies. Also cut pieces of colored construction paper into various geometric shapes (such as squares, rectangles, circles, and triangles). These shapes should have a writing area that is approximately 4x4 inches. Create one shape for each student.

Make sure students are divided into small groups (for more information on this, see p. 7), and take some time to study John 13 on your own.

worship idea

For your theme song for the weekend, use "Every Move I Make" from the two-CD set I Could Sing of Your Love Forever. For more information on ordering student lyrics books, a song leader book, and the CDs, call Group Publishing at 1-800-447-1070.

suggested schedule

2-Night Retreat

Day	Time	Activity	Supplies
Friday	6:00-7:00 p.m.	Games	
	7:00-8:00 p.m.	Teaching Session 1: Check, Please!	Bibles, dictionaries, thesauruses, concordances, cookies, cups, juice, aprons, butcher paper, markers
	8:00-9:30 p.m.	Free Time or Games	
	9:30-10:00 p.m.	Small-Group Discussion 1	Photocopies of "Small-Group Discussion 1" box (p. 81)
	10:00-10:30 p.m.	Snacks	
	11:00 p.m.	Lights Out	
Saturday	7:30-8:00 a.m.	Student Quiet Time 1: My Feet?!	Bibles, photocopies of "Student Quiet Time 1: *My Feet?!*" (p. 87), pencils or pens
	8:00-9:00 a.m.	Breakfast	
	9:00-10:00 a.m.	Teaching Session 2: My Serve!	Bibles, tennis racket, tennis balls
	10:00 a.m.-noon	Games or Group Activities	
	noon-1:00 p.m.	Lunch	
	1:00-3:00 p.m.	Free Time	
	3:00-4:00 p.m.	Teaching Session 3: See the Need	Bibles, pitcher, basin, small table, towel, magazines, newspapers, flyers, index cards, glue sticks, scissors, pencils or pens, paper
	4:00-5:00 p.m.	Free Time	
	5:00-6:00 p.m.	Dinner	
	6:00-9:30 p.m.	Games or Group Activities	
	9:30-10:00 p.m.	Small-Group Discussion 2	Photocopies of "Small-Group Discussion 2" box (p. 85)
	10:00-10:30 p.m.	Snacks	
	11:00 p.m.	Lights Out	
Sunday	7:30-8:00 a.m.	Student Quiet Time 2: Feelin' Good	Bibles, photocopies of "Student Quiet Time 2: Feelin' Good" (p. 88), pencils or pens
	8:00-9:00 a.m.	Breakfast	
	9:00-10:45 a.m.	Games or Group Activities	
	10:45 a.m.-noon	Teaching Session 4: Do Your Part	Bibles, garbage bags, cleaning supplies, construction paper, markers, glue sticks

Day	Time	Activity	Supplies
Friday	6:00-7:00 p.m.	Teaching Session 1: Check, Please!	Bibles, dictionaries, thesauruses, concordances, cookies, cups, juice, aprons, butcher paper, markers
	7:00-8:30 p.m.	Games	
	8:30-9:30 p.m.	Teaching Session 2: My Serve!	Bibles, tennis racket, tennis balls
	9:30-10:00 p.m.	Snacks	
	10:00-10:30 p.m.	Small-Group Discussion 1	Photocopies of "Small-Group Discussion 1" box (p. 81)
	11:00 p.m.	Lights Out	
Saturday	7:30-8:00 a.m.	Student Quiet Time 2: Feelin' Good	Bibles, photocopies of "Student Quiet Time 2: Feelin' Good" (p. 88), pencils or pens
	8:00-9:00 a.m.	Breakfast	
	9:00-10:00 a.m.	Teaching Session 3: See the Need	Bibles, pitcher, basin, small table, towel, magazines, newspapers, flyers, index cards, glue sticks, scissors, pencils or pens, paper
	10:00-10:45 a.m.	Free Time	
	10:45 a.m.-noon	Teaching Session 4: Do Your Part	Bibles, garbage bags, cleaning supplies, construction paper, markers, glue sticks

leader tip

You may want to begin each teaching session with five to ten minutes of singing. In addition to the suggested theme song, select other praise and worship songs that will complement the theme of the weekend.

teaching session 1: check, please!

Before the session, select four students who will serve cookies and juice to the rest of the teenagers. Explain to two of the servers that they are to be kind, considerate, humble, and friendly as they serve, even if the other students treat them rudely. Explain to the other two servers that they are to be distracted, rude, and inattentive as they serve. Give each of these four servers an apron to wear.

Begin the session by having all of the teenagers take a seat and explaining that four students will be serving them snacks. Instruct the servers to get started individually delivering a cookie and a cup of juice to each student. Once they've finished, thank them for their participation and have them take a seat.

Ask: • **Did you notice any differences between the ways you were served? Explain.**

• **Have you ever had very bad service at a restaurant? What was it like? What made it so bad?**

• **What about great service experiences?**

Say: **It's not difficult to picture what bad service looks like. You're at a restaurant and you wait an hour for your food, then when you get it, you realize it's not even what you ordered. Or you're in line at a store, and at the checkout you get charged for something you didn't even buy. Or maybe you've got bad cable service, where the picture is always fuzzy or all the people are green.**

But what is good service? Real and true service is *much* more than getting your food on time at a restaurant or being smiled at in a grocery store.

Have students form trios, and challenge each group to come up with a short definition of the word *service*. Encourage them to use Bibles, dictionaries, thesauruses, and concordances as they create their definitions. Once they come to a unanimous decision on their definition, each trio should use a marker to write it on the butcher paper on the wall. Tell students that they'll be using the paper banner throughout the weekend, so they should leave lots of blank space remaining on the banner.

After all the groups have written their definitions, have the students gather back together in a large group, and invite a student to read John 13:1-17 aloud. Say: **Jesus took on the role of a lowly servant by washing his disciples' feet. That's amazing—the God of the universe stooping to that level to show his love. But what's even more amazing is that he did it on the very night he was arrested. It was his last night with his disciples, his closest friends—it was his chance to teach them some really important stuff! So he chose to teach them the importance of service.**

Ask: • **What amazes you most about this story?**

• **How do you think the disciples felt when Jesus washed their feet?**

• **If you were there, how would you have felt?**

• **In your opinion, why did Jesus do it?**

Have students take a few minutes in their trios to re-evaluate their definitions of service. Encourage them to add to or modify their definitions based on what they read in John 13.

After all the groups have finished editing their definitions, close by encouraging the students to mingle around the poster, reading all of the definitions written there.

small-group discussion 1

Discuss these questions in your small group:

• Have you ever been involved in a service project (such as volunteering, going on a missions trip, or helping with a food drive)? Share your experience.

• What should someone's attitude be when they serve?

• Have you ever tried to serve or help someone and they've treated you rudely? How did it make you feel? Explain.

• As Christians, what should motivate us to serve other people, even when they "don't deserve it"? Explain.

teaching session 2: my serve!

Ask students to name some famous professional tennis players. Then ask students to shout out some of the basic principles and rules of the game. Ask if any of the students know what an "ace" is in tennis, and if so, invite them to explain it to the others.

Say: **An ace is a serve that hits the mark. It's the perfect serve. It accomplishes its purpose. If a tennis player were able to ace every serve, he or she could win a tournament, hands down.**

That's how we want to serve. We want our service to hit the mark—to make a difference.

Take the tennis balls you previously prepared, and use the tennis racket to lob them (underhand) into the air for students to catch. After all six balls have been distributed, have the students form six even groups—each group should have one of the tennis balls.

Encourage the groups to spread out around the room and read the Bible verses written on their tennis balls. Groups should discuss the verses, focusing on the following questions:

- **What role does God play in service?**

- **Who or what should service focus on?**

After about two minutes of discussion time, have each group toss its ball to another group and then discuss its new verse. This should be repeated until each group has read all six Scripture passages.

for younger teenagers

To prevent potential injuries caused by torpedoing tennis balls, instruct younger teenagers to send runners between each group as a way to pass the tennis balls.

When all of the verses have been read, have groups discuss these questions:

- **Is it easy or hard to live out these verses? Explain.**

- **How can focusing on God motivate someone to serve, even in really tough situations? Give examples.**

- **Why does God want us to serve others?**

- **What's dangerous about living a life just focused on yourself?**

Say: **There are lots of people in the world who serve others. They feed the poor. They provide clothes for the needy. They visit the sick and dying. They give money to charity. But *why* do they do it? Some people do it because of guilt— they feel compelled to help others because their own health or success makes them feel guilty. Some people do it out of a sense of duty—it's just something they "have" to do to be a good citizen. Some people do it to impress others—to**

leader tip

Need game ideas? Check out the game book suggestions on page 7!

make sure everybody else knows how kind and generous they are. Some people do it just to make themselves feel good—they like the sense of satisfaction they have after their hard work. And of course, some people don't do it at all.

As Christians, we serve others as a way to serve God. It's not to impress others, it's not because of guilt or duty, and it shouldn't be just to make ourselves feel good (because sometimes serving others *doesn't* feel good).

But when we focus on serving our Lord, we can do it. We can get the energy. We can find the motivation. We have a purpose.

Have groups look up the Scriptures written on their tennis balls one more time, and encourage them to each use the verse to create a prayer and pray together in their groups.

teaching session 3: see the need

Before this session begins, set up a small table near the door with a pitcher of water, a basin, and a towel.

Begin by encouraging the students to imagine what it might have been like the night Jesus washed the disciples' feet. Prompt them to imagine the sounds of the conversation and the smells of the food. Ask each student to imagine that he or she is one of the disciples, ready for a special meal with Jesus.

Say: **Picture the disciples walking into the room. Some are talking, some are laughing, some are probably very hungry.**

Perhaps some of them noticed, though, that the servant who was to wash their feet (an evening meal tradition) was missing. Some may have gone on without paying any attention, but others might have grumbled. They had walked a lot that day—they were tired…their feet were dusty.

Point to the table you set up by the doorway with the pitcher, basin, and towel. Say: **If you were there, what would you have done?** (Pause.) **Would you have ignored the need and kept on talking? Would you have maybe complained about it?** (Pause.)

Do you ever wonder why one of the disciples didn't jump up and offer to wash the others' feet?

Jesus saw the need—and the opportunity. Jesus saw more than a basin of water and a towel—he saw a chance to meet needs, to impact lives, to teach a deep and life-changing lesson.

Have students form trios with the same students from their groups in Teaching Session 1 and discuss the following questions:

• **We don't know all the details of what happened that night, but we do know that before any of the disciples offered to do anything, Jesus chose to wash the**

leader tip

To help set the mood for this session, dim the lights in the meeting area and set up a few candles. Use a worship or instrumental CD for quiet background music.

others' feet. What may have been some of the reasons that the disciples either didn't see or didn't respond to this need?

• **Do you ever "walk by" needs without noticing them or doing something about them? Explain.**

Pass out some magazines, newspapers, and flyers from local charities to each trio along with a pair of scissors, a glue stick, pencils or pens, and paper for taking notes. Challenge trios to each take twenty minutes to look through the material you've passed out and use it to identify five specific needs, either in the local community or in the world (such as homelessness, hunger, or a local charity's financial needs). After they have identified five needs, challenge them to come up with general ideas for ways those needs can be met. Encourage trios to conclude by narrowing down their focus to only one specific need that they think they can do something about.

Have students use scissors to cut out some pictures or words that represent the needs they are focusing on. Students should then glue their pictures and words onto the banner on the wall, trying not to cover over the definitions of service already written there.

Once each trio has added its need to the banner, invite a few volunteers to share the needs their trio discussed and some of their ideas for addressing those needs.

Ask: • **Do all of these needs seem overwhelming to you? Like it's too hard to make a difference? Why or why not?**

• **What are some specific ideas you have of ways we can personally, or as a group, serve others in some of these need areas?**

• **How can trying to meet these needs be a way to serve God? Be specific.**

Pass out index cards and pens or pencils and have students form their trios again. Challenge them to discuss the possibilities and to each write down one specific step they will commit to take, either as a team or individually, to address the need their trio is focusing on.

Conclude by inviting a student to read John 13:1-17 aloud. Encourage students to take at least five minutes to pray silently about seeing needs in the world. Encourage them to use the banner on the wall and the basin of water by the door as prayer symbols, representing their commitments. Tell them that they may kneel by the banner or in front of the table with the pitcher and basin. If they'd like, they could even put a hand on the banner or on the items at the table to represent their desire to meet the needs God has placed on their hearts.

leader tip

Remind students that these should be achievable action steps. Instead of writing "help the homeless" or "end to poverty," encourage students to come up with steps like "use part of my allowance to buy canned food for our church's food pantry" or "visit the local nursing home and talk to lonely patients."

small-group discussion 2

Discuss these questions in your small group:

· *Is it possible to respond to all the needs you see in the world? Why or why not?*

· *How can you determine which need (or needs) to focus on?*

· *What need have you decided to focus on, and what action step did you commit to take?*

· *How will you need God's strength and help to address the need you are focusing on?*

teaching session 4: do your part

Begin by sharing with the students how proud you are of the commitments and action steps they discussed in the last teaching session. Encourage them in their commitments!

Say: **There are lots of big needs in the world and in our community—lots of hurting people. I'm so excited about how God is going to use you to address those needs! You are going to be stretched and challenged in amazing ways!**

Pass out garbage bags and cleaning supplies to the students, and say: **But serving others isn't always dramatic and exciting. A lot of times it means doing the stinky jobs, like Jesus did, without getting any praise or thanks for it.**

Invite a student to read John 13:14-15 aloud, and say: **We're going to follow Jesus' example and do some "stinky" jobs today. Not because it is fun or exciting, but because we can honor God by serving others and taking care of our environment.**

Divide students into various crews to tackle the jobs appropriate for your location, such as a grounds clean-up crew, a window-washing crew, a kitchen clean-up crew, or even a toilet-scrubbing crew. Tell the teenagers that they'll have only thirty minutes to work as hard as they can on their crews, and challenge them to consider it an act of service to God.

When time is up, gather the students back together and help them to debrief their experience. Ask:

• **What did you do and what was it like?**

• **What was the worst part of your job?**

• **Was it easy or challenging to see your act of service as a way to worship God? Explain.**

• How can serving others through "little things" like cleaning affect other people's lives?

Pass out markers and the construction paper shapes you prepared, and encourage the students to each brainstorm one "little thing" they can do in their everyday life to serve others. These need to be things that are not part of their regular chores—they should be extra ways to serve family members, friends, or even strangers (such as picking up trash, setting the dinner table, or writing a nice note to a teacher).

Students should write down their ideas and then use glue to add their shapes to the banner of pictures and words that is hanging on the wall.

Say: **Together we've created a mosaic of service! This banner represents all we've learned—all God has put on our hearts.**

Give students a few minutes to mingle around the banner, reading and observing all that they've studied and discussed over the weekend.

End the retreat by commissioning the students for service in the world. Have them all stand in front of the banner and put one hand on it to symbolize their commitment. Read John 13:12-17 to the students, and close by praying for them, asking God to empower them as they strive to serve others.

At the end of the retreat, roll up the banner and take it with you to hang in the youth room as a visual reminder of what the group has studied.

Student Quiet Time 1:

My Feet?!

Take off your shoes and your socks. Don't worry, no one is close enough to smell them…except you. Look at your feet. Imagine Jesus washing them—pouring water over one and then the other as a way to show you his love. How would you react? Would you be embarrassed or shy? Resistant? Uncomfortable?

Read John 13:5-9.

Simon Peter wasn't sure how to respond to Jesus' act of service. It was so humble and unheard of that it caught Peter off guard. But when he understood that accepting Jesus' service—accepting his love—was an essential part of being Jesus' follower, he enthusiastically received Jesus' gift.

How has God served you? Loved you? Blessed you? How do these gifts make you feel? How do you respond?

Could you be like Jesus? Could you touch, wash, and probably *smell* the worst parts of people? Are you willing to sacrifice your own comfort to serve others?

Pray, telling God your feelings about serving others. What is holding you back? Be honest. How do you want to grow in this area? Tell him what you really feel.

Student Quiet Time 2:
Feelin' Good

"I just love visiting the old people in the nursing home. It makes me feel so good afterward!"

"Why did I give food in the food drive? To feel like I'm making a difference."

"I'm so glad to have been a part of this project and to have raised money to feed the homeless. It's something I can really be proud of."

Do you see anything wrong with these statements? Read them again.

Where's the focus?

Me…me…me.

So often we serve others to make ourselves feel good. To alleviate guilt. To fulfill our duty. To make ourselves proud.

These reasons may sound good, but they're not. They're wrong. They take the focus off God and his love for people and put it on us and our love for ourselves.

Do you feel motivated to serve others? If you don't, just be honest. What do you feel and why?

Think of the last time you served someone else, but didn't feel appreciated. Did it upset or disappoint you? What does that tell you about your motivations?

On the back of this paper, list all of the things that motivate you to serve. When you've finished, cross out all of the motives that have the wrong focus. Read Ephesians 6:7, then pray that God will help you serve with the right motivation—serving and worshipping him.

risk-taking faith

retreat focus: Students will consider the examples of Daniel, Shadrach, Meshach, and Abednego—four men who exemplified risk-taking faith.

retreat motto: Leap before you look.

theme verse: "And without faith it is impossible to please God, because anyone who comes to him must believe that he exists and that he rewards those who earnestly seek him" (Hebrews 11:6).

preparation

Before the retreat, gather all of the necessary supplies and make all of the photocopies recommended in the Master Supply List.

For Teaching Session 1, cue up *M:I-2* by setting the VCR counter at 0:00:00 when the studio logo appears before the movie starts. The segment you'll show starts at approximately 0:06:00 when Ethan Hunt is rock climbing.

Make sure students are divided into small groups (for more information on this, see p. 7), and take some time to study Daniel 1–3 on your own.

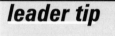

leader tip

Avoid the embarrassment of showing the wrong scene—preview movie clips before using them!

worship idea

For your theme song for the weekend, use "You're Worthy of My Praise" from the two-CD set *I Could Sing of Your Love Forever*. For information on ordering student lyrics books, a song leader book, and the CDs, call Group at 1-800-447-1070.

master supply list

In addition to basic retreat supplies such as food, games, Bibles, pens, pencils, paper, and worship music, you'll also need the following supplies:

- ❏ *Mission: Impossible II (M:I-2)* video (or DVD)
- ❏ VCR (or DVD player)
- ❏ TV
- ❏ 2 pieces of poster board or newsprint
- ❏ 1 photocopy of "Small-Group Discussion 1" box (p. 93) for each small group
- ❏ 1 photocopy of "Student Quiet Time 1: Is This the God I Know?" (p. 99) for each student
- ❏ 1 photocopy of "Small-Group Discussion 2" box (p. 96) for each small group
- ❏ 1 photocopy of "Student Quiet Time 2: SFS" (p. 100) for each student
- ❏ 1 large cookie for each pair of students
- ❏ 1 American dollar bill for each student
- ❏ markers

suggested schedule

2-Night Retreat

Day	Time	Activity	Supplies
Friday	6:00-7:00 p.m.	Games	
	7:00-8:00 p.m.	Teaching Session 1: Mission Possible or Impossible?	*M:I-2* video, VCR, TV, poster board or newsprint, markers
	8:00-9:30 p.m.	Free Time or Games	
	9:30-10:00 p.m.	Small-Group Discussion 1	Photocopies of "Small-Group Discussion 1" box (p. 93)
	10:00-10:30 p.m.	Snacks	
	11:00 p.m.	Lights Out	
Saturday	7:30-8:00 a.m.	Student Quiet Time 1: Is This the God I Know?	Bibles, photocopies of "Student Quiet Time 1: Is This the God I Know?" (p. 99), pencils or pens
	8:00-9:00 a.m.	Breakfast	
	9:00-10:00 a.m.	Teaching Session 2: Evidence Room	Bibles
	10:00 a.m.-noon	Games or Group Activities	
	noon-1:00 p.m.	Lunch	
	1:00-3:00 p.m.	Free Time	
	3:00-4:00 p.m.	Teaching Session 3: Act One, Scene One	Bibles
	4:00-5:00 p.m.	Free Time	
	5:00-6:00 p.m.	Dinner	
	6:00-9:30 p.m.	Games or Group Activities	
	9:30-10:00 p.m.	Small-Group Discussion 2	Photocopies of "Small-Group Discussion 2" box (p. 96)
	10:00-10:30 p.m.	Snacks	
	11:00 p.m.	Lights Out	
Sunday	7:30-8:00 a.m.	Student Quiet Time 2: SFS	Bibles, photocopies of "Student Quiet Time 2: SFS" (p. 100), pencils or pens
	8:00-9:00 a.m.	Breakfast	
	9:00-10:00 a.m.	Teaching Session 4: No Compromise	Large cookies, pencils, paper
	10:00-11:00 a.m.	Worship Session: In God We Trust	American dollar bills, poster board or newsprint, markers
	11:00 a.m.-noon	Games or Group Activities	

Day	Time	Activity	Supplies
Friday	6:00-7:00 p.m.	Teaching Session 2: Evidence Room	Bibles
	7:00-8:30 p.m.	Games	
	8:30-9:30 p.m.	Teaching Session 3: Act One, Scene One	Bibles
	9:30-10:00 p.m.	Snacks	
	10:00-10:30 p.m.	Small-Group Discussion 1	Photocopies of "Small-Group Discussion 1" box (p. 93)
	11:00 p.m.	Lights Out	
Saturday	7:30-8:00 a.m.	Student Quiet Time 2: SFS	Bibles, photocopies of "Student Quiet Time 2: SFS" (p. 100), pencils or pens
	8:00-9:00 a.m.	Breakfast	
	9:00-10:00 a.m.	Games or Group Activities	
	10:00-11:00 a.m.	Teaching Session 4: No Compromise	Large cookies, pencils, paper
	11:00 a.m.-noon	Worship Session: In God We Trust	American dollar bills, poster board or newsprint, markers

teaching session 1: mission possible or impossible?

Show the *M:I-2* segment that features Ethan Hunt rock climbing, beginning at approximately 0:06:00. When the counter reaches approximately 0:07:25, Hunt will leap from one outcrop over to another outcrop—in slow motion. Pause the movie at that point, in mid-jump.

Say: **Let's rate your degree of confidence that Ethan Hunt is going to survive the jump he's making. Rate your confidence from 1 to 10. A number 1 rating means you think it's time to call for a body bag—there's no *way* he's going to make it. A number 10 rating means you think it's a piece of cake. You have absolutely no doubt he'll pull through.**

Count from one to ten, keeping track on a piece of poster board or newsprint how many votes each number collects.

Then repeat the process, asking your teenagers to rank their confidence that an athletic teenager in your group could safely complete the jump. Use a specific athlete as an example. Keep track of the votes in a different color marker, and place them next to the votes Ethan received.

Repeat the process again, this time asking your teenagers to rank their confidence that a specific adult volunteer could safely complete the jump. Keep track of the votes in a third color of marker and place them next to the votes Ethan and the athlete received.

Summarize how students have voted for all three people, and state which person they appear to have the most confidence in.

Roll the remainder of the clip. Play the tape through the moment Ethan emerges on top of the mountain and looks around, about 0:08:20 on the counter.

Ask: • **How many of you knew he'd make it? Why?**

Say: **In this movie, Tom Cruise plays the character Ethan Hunt, a secret agent—so he can do anything, right? We've got a *lot* of confidence in him. Plus, since he's the star of the movie, it's not likely the producers will drop Tom Cruise off a cliff in the first few minutes of the film.**

Explain to your students this basic risk-assessment principle: The greater a person's ability to do something, or the more confidence a person has in the person helping him or her do something, the less risky the behavior is. Share several examples of this principle with your students. For example, you could compare an expert downhill skier going down a black diamond slope to a beginning skier attempting the same run. Obviously there is less risk of injury for the expert. Another example you could share is going white-water rafting with a guide as compared to going it alone; with a guide in the raft, the risk is greatly reduced.

Ask teenagers to form trios and discuss:

• **How confident would you be of your own ability to make the jump Ethan Hunt made in the film clip we watched? Why?**

• **Describe a time you did something that was physically risky for you. What was it? How did you feel?**

• **What's something you can do that might seem risky to others but is easy for you?**

Ask for volunteers to share any stories they heard in their trios that stand out as particularly risky. After students have shared, ask trios to try to define the term "calculated risk." Invite several trios to share their responses, then summarize the meaning of the term by pointing out that a calculated risk is when someone does something risky and exciting, but usually only things the person is sure he or she will live through because of skill or because of help from a trusted source.

Say: **God asks us to have a risk-taking faith—to move outside our comfort zones and do things to serve others that we can't do on our own, to follow God into places that cause us to rely on him. Risk-taking faith isn't for the weak of heart. It stretches us.**

During our retreat we'll consider what risk-taking faith looked like in the life of a man named Daniel, and in the lives of three government employees who decided to say no to a king.

small-group discussion 1

Discuss these questions in your small group:

· *Tonight we talked about taking risks. On a 1 to 10 scale, with number 10 being "show me a cliff and I'll jump off it" and number 1 being "I wear a helmet at all times in case of falling meteorites," what number best represents you? What's the riskiest thing you've done lately?*

· *Is faith risky? What are some challenges and risks involved in being a Christian?*

· *When have you had to take a risk in your faith? Explain.*

teaching session 2: evidence room

Ask your students to form three groups that are approximately the same size. Instruct the groups to circle up and sit far enough apart that they can read Daniel 1:1—2:23 aloud without disturbing the other groups.

Be sure each group has at least one Bible, and allow up to five minutes for groups to thoroughly read the passage aloud.

When the reading is done, assemble the groups in one place. Ask kids to sit in their groups and summarize the following information about Daniel's story: Daniel was a young man who was in the royal court of Israel. Babylon invaded and the Babylonian king kidnapped some of Israel's brightest and best—including Daniel. They had three years to be trained in all things Babylonian, and then they'd enter the king's service. Daniel led a request to eat vegetarian rather than enjoy the rich foods from the king's table. He and his friends did well in the program, and when the king questioned them, they were ten times better than the magicians and enchanters in Babylon. Plus, Daniel could understand visions and dreams of all kinds.

This turned out to be a handy skill when the king had a disturbing dream. The king asked his assembled wise men to not only interpret the dream, but to describe what the dream was, too. When the wise men argued that this was an impossible task, the king ordered his guards to round up the wise men and have them killed. Daniel went to the king and asked for a little time, which was granted. And Daniel and his friends then prayed that God would reveal the content and meaning of the king's dream to them. The good news: God did reveal the dream in a vision that Daniel experienced.

Let student groups add any details they think are important that you skipped over. When groups have finished, ask a volunteer to read Daniel 2:19-23 aloud. Next ask that

leader tip

Need game ideas? Check out the game book suggestions on page 7!

a volunteer reader from each group stand and that one of them read verse 20, another read verse 21, and a final reader read verse 22.

Say: **These verses express what Daniel believed about God. They reveal the confidence Daniel had in the help he was getting from God as he lived his life.**

Ask the kids in each group to answer the following questions as they consider the verse their reader read aloud:

- **What evidence is there that God deserves this reputation?**

- **What evidence is there that God *doesn't* deserve this reputation?**

for younger teenagers

The personal vulnerability called for in answering these two questions—especially suggesting reasons that God hasn't earned an excellent reputation—may be a challenge for younger teenagers who are eager to please you.

If you have a high number of young teenagers, consider softening the questions a bit. Use these questions instead:

- ***Why do you think God deserves a good reputation?***

- ***Why might someone not think well of God?***

After groups wrap up their conversations, have everyone assemble together. Ask each small group to sum up its conclusions, and invite discussion about the findings, encouraging students to address one another's concerns.

Conclude the session by prompting small groups to spend a few minutes praying together about what they've learned so far.

teaching session 3: act one, scene one

Say: **Congratulations! You're now professional actors who are about to take the stage. The good news is that you have no lines to learn. But you *will* have to act out the epic story that's about to unfold.**

Cast the following roles: King Nebuchadnezzar, Satraps, Governors, Provincial Officials, Golden Image, Shadrach, Meshach, Strongest Soldiers, and Abednego.

Because the Bible text is unclear about the number of officials and soldiers involved in this incident, place the bulk of your teenagers in these roles. Involve everyone! Don't have an audience; your teenagers will learn more if they *experience* the Bible text rather than *watch* it experienced.

Instruct your actors to act along with the story as it unfolds. Read Daniel 3:1-30 aloud (or recruit a capable volunteer to read it).

As you begin, place the Golden Image at center stage. Place the King, Satraps, Governors, Strongest Soldiers, and Provincial Officials on one side of the stage; place Shadrach, Meshach, and Abednego on the other side of the stage.

After acting out the text—which is a straightforward narrative—have the teenagers form trios that, as much as possible, include a variety of characters. Have trios discuss the following questions:

• **From the perspective of the character you played in this historical drama, in what ways did Shadrach, Meshach, and Abednego express their faith in God?**

• **What risks did the three government employees take to stand up for their faith?**

• **Can you think of any situations in our world today that might parallel the situation faced by the three government employees?**

Say: **Shadrach, Meshach, and Abednego got out of their situation alive. But having faith in God isn't a guarantee that you'll coast through life without problems or that God will always rescue you. Being a Christian and living a faithful, obedient life actually sets you up for conflict with your culture. You can *expect* it.**

Note what our three heroes said in chapter 3, verses 16-18.

Ask a volunteer to read the passage aloud, then ask: • **How do you think Shadrach, Meshach, and Abednego felt when their lives were in big danger?**

• **What strikes you about their faith?**

Say: **Their faith in God wasn't about God saving their bodies from the flames. They knew that God was ultimately right, and they decided to faithfully obey God no matter what.**

Remind your students of the risk-assessment principle from the first session: The greater a person's ability to do something, or the more confidence a person has in the person helping him or her do something, the less risky the behavior is. Ask teenagers to share their thoughts about how this principle relates to the actions of Shadrach, Meshach, and Abednego.

Ask: • **In your opinion, were Shadrach, Meshach, and Abednego showing a risk-taking faith as they walked toward the furnace? Defend your opinion.**

After several students have shared their ideas, say: **Were they showing risk-taking faith? Yes and no. They were taking a risk with their bodies, but their souls were never in jeopardy. They knew who they were following and who was helping them. That took all the risk out of the situation.**

Close by having students prayerfully reflect on the following questions:

• **What risks are we willing to take as a group to follow God in a radical way?**

• **What risks are you willing to take?**

leader tip

The passage your teenagers will act out mentions a long list of Persian government officials—including "satraps." What's a satrap?

A satrap was a ruling official in the Persian empire. A satrap's jurisdiction extended across more than one province, which made a satrap essentially a deputy king.

small-group discussion 2

Discuss these questions in your small group:

· Suppose today was the first time you heard the story of King Nebuchadnezzar, Shadrach, Meshach, and Abednego. Can you think of a slogan that would fit on a bumper sticker that sums up the moral of the story?

· If you could show your faith in God through one really big act (like the fiery furnace) or through a bunch of daily little acts (such as telling friends about Jesus or giving money to church), which would you choose? Which is hardest? Why?

· Think of something that your friends might do that you think you can't do and still serve God. What would that be? How would you respond if asked to participate?

teaching session 4: no compromise

Ask teenagers to form pairs with someone they haven't yet been with in a discussion group. Give each pair a cookie. Explain that you want them to assume they're all desperately hungry—*starving*, in fact. But before they touch the cookie, ask pairs to discuss these questions:

• **What's the fairest way to split the cookie between you?**

• **In your family, what's the technique used to divide up something that everyone wants—such as a cookie or time controlling the TV remote?**

Ask for volunteers to share their suggestions for making things fair. When you've fielded and affirmed four or five comments, ask pairs to divide up their cookies and enjoy them as you speak.

Ask for a few student volunteers to create their own definitions for the word *compromise*. Next ask several volunteers to share personal examples of everyday situations that call for a compromise (such as giving up one's right to the TV remote so there's some peace in the living room or giving up one's pride in order to keep a relationship).

Explain to the students that although compromising is a valuable life skill, when it comes to trusting and following God, compromise isn't necessarily a good thing. Daniel didn't compromise. Shadrach, Meshach, and Abednego certainly didn't compromise. They followed. Period.

Say: **When it comes to trusting God and following him, there's no room for compromise. Even if it seems risky, you go where you're sent. You do what you're told to do. You listen and obey.**

In your pairs, discuss the following questions:

- **Describe a time you risked something to obey God. What happened?**

- **If you were willing to risk everything—your popularity, your security, and your significance—to follow God, what do you think God would ask you to do?**

- **If you have a clear answer to the question I just asked—why haven't you done it? What's standing in your way?**

- **What's a "next step" you can take to live out a risk-taking faith in God?**

Distribute a piece of paper and a pencil to each teenager.

Say: **Good intentions are just that: intentions. Change and risk-taking faith require action. With your partner, please think through the next step you identified, and turn it into a commitment—a commitment you'll put in writing. For example, if you said you'll obey God by admitting to a teacher that you plagiarized a paper, write down *who* you'll talk with, *where* you'll be, and *when* it will happen. Be specific—the more specific the better.**

When a few minutes have passed, ask pairs of teenagers to pray together about their action steps, asking for the courage to act on their risk-taking faith.

Ask teenagers to take their commitment papers with them—and to check in with their partners about how the risk-taking faith "next steps" turned out.

worship session: in god we trust

Distribute a crisp, new, American one-dollar bill to each of your teenagers. Point out where it says, "In God We Trust" on the back of the bill.

Say: **Let's talk about us here—do we trust God? *Really* trust God?**

Our trust in God lets us live out a risk-taking faith. It's what assures us that God will care for us even if we're cut to pieces by an angry king or even if the furnace turns us into toast.

Prompt teenagers to think about their own trust in God. Then instruct them to find some way to turn their dollar bill into a symbol of trust in God (without ripping the paper bill). Give them ten minutes to think about and then create their symbols.

Encourage kids to move about the room as they wish, to create a space in which they can think, pray, meditate, and create.

When ten minutes have passed, offer the opportunity for teenagers to share and explain their creations. Be sensitive to the power of this moment—you may hear unexpected things from individuals who have deepened in their faith at this retreat. Be deliberately open and affirming. Encourage students who take the risk of sharing what they're feeling. Don't tolerate mockery or snickering.

Say: **God works first *in* us, and then *through* us. Please form trios and together discuss your answer to the following question.**

Ask: • **Since you get to keep this dollar, how will you spend it in a way that communicates a radical, risk-taking faith in God? Generate as many suggestions as you can in five minutes.**

Answers may include: Buy a school outcast a coke and strike up a conversation; give it personally to a soup kitchen and also offer to work there for an hour; carry it in your wallet and the next time someone at school complains about not having enough money, give it to that person.

Ask trios to share their ideas. Jot down the ideas on a piece of poster board or newsprint. When you've collected all the ideas your group has to offer, pray for each person to have faith to turn one of the suggestions into reality. Invite kids to hold up their dollar bills as together you commit the dollar bills—and yourselves—to God's service.

Is This the God I Know?

Read Daniel 2:19-22.

Do I believe this is all true? Daniel certainly did, but that was Daniel—and I'm me. When I read these words and think about how I've experienced God in my life, do I agree with Daniel? Or not? What do I believe about this God I'm supposed to trust?

It's no wonder Daniel was willing to take risks—he trusted God absolutely. In what ways do I trust God? In what ways am I unsure?

If I trusted God like Daniel trusted God, how would that change how I act at school? at home? at this retreat?

Am I satisfied with my relationship with God? In what ways do I want to see it change during this retreat?

Student Quiet Time 2: # SFS*

Read Daniel 3:16-18.

God doesn't owe me an easy life. He doesn't owe me health, wealth, or happiness. And he certainly doesn't owe me an explanation when things aren't going my way.

All of which makes it hard sometimes to trust him. Sometimes I suffer from SFS—***Selective Faith Syndrome.*** I trust when it's easy. But sometimes I don't know what he's up to…why things happen the way they happen…what's coming at me in the future.

God asks me to obey him—no matter what. To trust him—no matter what. To love him—no matter what.

Even as I'm walking toward the furnace.

If I had been standing on the sidelines as Shadrach and his friends walked by, heading toward the furnace, here's what I'd have thought:

_____

_____

_____

_____

Here's how I feel about trusting God with my future:

_____

_____

_____

_____

If someone watching me was asked if I live in a way that shows I trust God, here's what that person would answer:

_____

_____

_____

_____

And here's the evidence that person would point to in my life:

_____

_____

_____

_____

*Selective Faith Syndrome

road trip

retreat focus: Students will study the loyal friendship of Ruth and Naomi and will explore ways they can express that loyalty in their relationships with others.

retreat motto: We all need somebody to lean on.

theme verse: "Let love and faithfulness never leave you; bind them around your neck, write them on the tablet of your heart" (Proverbs 3:3).

preparation

Before the retreat, gather all of the necessary supplies and make all of the photocopies recommended in the Master Supply List.

For Teaching Session 1, cue up *Toy Story* by setting the VCR counter at 0:00:00 when the studio logo appears before the movie starts. The segment you'll show starts at approximately 1:07:00 when Woody says, "Nice work." Cue up *Toy Story 2* in the same way, by setting the counter at 0:00:00 when the studio logo appears and then fast-forwarding to approximately 1:04:05 when Buzz Lightyear says, "Woody, you're in danger."

For Teaching Session 2, look up Proverbs 3:3 in several different Bible translations and write the versions of the verse on large pieces of poster board, indicating which translation or paraphrase it is from at the bottom of the poster. You may want to include the New International Version, King James Version, New American Standard Bible, New Living Translation, and *The Message*. Also, use sharp scissors to cut each of the craft sticks in half.

> ### leader tip
>
> Avoid the embarrassment of showing the wrong scene— preview movie clips before using them!

For Teaching Session 4, cut a piece of yarn (approximately eight to ten inches long) for each student. Use a hole punch to put a hole in the corner of one index card for each student.

Make sure students are divided into small groups (for more information on this, see p. 7), and take some time to study the book of Ruth on your own.

worship idea

For your theme song for the weekend, use "What a Friend I've Found" from the two-CD set *I Could Sing of Your Love Forever*. For information on ordering student lyrics books, a song leader book, and the CDs, call Group at 1-800-447-1070.

master supply list

In addition to basic retreat supplies such as food, games, Bibles, pens, pencils, paper, and worship music, you'll also need the following supplies:

- ❏ *Toy Story* video (or DVD)
- ❏ *Toy Story 2* video (or DVD)
- ❏ VCR (or DVD player)
- ❏ TV
- ❏ dry-erase board
- ❏ dry-erase markers
- ❏ several pieces of poster board
- ❏ 1 photocopy of "Small-Group Discussion 1" box (p. 104) for each small group
- ❏ 1 photocopy of "Student Quiet Time 1: Signs" (p. 110) for each student
- ❏ 1 craft stick for each student
- ❏ hot glue guns
- ❏ several skeins of yarn
- ❏ colored markers
- ❏ 1 photocopy of "Dear Abby" handout (p. 112) cut into rectangles
- ❏ 1 photocopy of "Small-Group Discussion 2" box (p. 107) for each small group
- ❏ 1 photocopy of "Student Quiet Time 2: Circle of Friends" (p. 111) for each student
- ❏ 1 photocopy of "Instant Message" handout (p. 113) for each student
- ❏ 1 index card for each student
- ❏ optional: artificial tree

suggested schedule

2-Night Retreat

Day	Time	Activity	Supplies
Friday	6:00-7:00 p.m.	Games	
	7:00-8:00 p.m.	Teaching Session 1: You've Got a Friend in Me	Bibles, TV, VCR, *Toy Story* video, *Toy Story 2* video
	8:00-9:30 p.m.	Free Time	
	9:30-10:00 p.m.	Small-Group Discussion 1	Photocopies of "Small-Group Discussion 1" box (p. 104)
	10:00-10:30 p.m.	Snacks	
	11:00 p.m.	Lights Out	
Saturday	7:30-8:00 a.m.	Student Quiet Time 1: Signs	Bibles, photocopies of "Student Quiet Time 1: Signs" handout (p. 110), pencils or pens
	8:00-9:00 a.m.	Breakfast	
	9:00-10:00 a.m.	Games or Group Activities	
	10:00-11:00 a.m.	Teaching Session 2: Heart Carving	Bibles, craft sticks, hot glue guns, yarn or string, markers, Proverbs 3:3 posters
	11:00 a.m.-noon	Free Time	
	noon-1:00 p.m.	Lunch	
	1:00-5:00 p.m.	Free Time or Group Activities	
	5:00-6:00 p.m.	Dinner	
	6:00-7:30 p.m.	Teaching Session 3: Dear Abby	Bibles, photocopy of "Dear Abby" handout cut into rectangles (p. 112)
	7:30-9:30 p.m.	Games or Group Activities	
	9:30-10:00 p.m.	Small-Group Discussion 2	Photocopies of "Small-Group Discussion 2" box (p. 107)
	10:00-10:30 p.m.	Snacks	
	11:00 p.m.	Lights Out	
Sunday	7:30-8:00 a.m.	Student Quiet Time 2: Circle of Friends	Bibles, photocopies of "Student Quiet Time 2: Circle of Friends" (p. 111), pencils or pens
	8:00-9:00 a.m.	Breakfast	
	9:00-10:00 a.m.	Teaching Session 4: A True Friend	Bibles, dry-erase board, dry-erase markers, photocopies of "Instant Message" handout (p. 113), pencils or pens, index cards
	10:00-10:30 a.m.	Worship Session: Strong Branches	Markers, yarn, tree (real or artificial)
	10:30 a.m.-noon	Games or Free Time	

1-Night Retreat

Day	Time	Activity	Supplies
Friday	6:00-7:00 p.m.	Games	
	7:00-8:00 p.m.	Teaching Session 1: You've Got a Friend in Me	Bibles, TV, VCR, *Toy Story* video, *Toy Story 2* video
	8:00-9:30 p.m.	Free Time	
	9:30-10:00 p.m.	Small-Group Discussion 1	Photocopies of "Small-Group Discussion 1" box (p. 104)
	10:00-10:30 p.m.	Snacks	
	11:00 p.m.	Lights Out	
Saturday	7:30-8:00 a.m.	Student Quiet Time 2: Circle of Friends	Bibles, photocopies of "Student Quiet Time 2: Circle of Friends" (p. 111), pencils or pens
	8:00-9:00 a.m.	Breakfast	
	9:00-10:00 a.m.	Teaching Session 4: A True Friend	Bibles, dry-erase board, dry-erase markers, photocopies of "Instant Message" handout (p. 113), pencils or pens, index cards
	10:00-10:30 a.m.	Worship Session: Strong Branches	Markers, yarn, tree (real or artificial)
	10:30 a.m.-noon	Games or Free Time	

teaching session 1: you've got a friend in me

Challenge your group to brainstorm as many "famous friendships" as they can, such as Charlie Brown and Snoopy, Batman and Robin, the friends on *Friends*, or Ruth and Naomi.

Invite a student to read Ruth 1:1-18 aloud. Say: **Ruth and Naomi had a great friendship. Part of what we will be talking about this weekend is what makes a good friendship. We're going to start by looking at some friends you may have seen before.**

Play the video clip from *Toy Story* beginning at approximately 1:07:00 when Woody says, "Nice work." Stop the video at approximately 1:10:50 when Woody is tossed out of the moving truck.

Ask: • **Woody and Buzz both have a chance to leave and save themselves, but neither will go without the other. How is this similar to the friendship of Ruth and Naomi?**

Have students form trios. Have one student in each group read Proverbs 17:17 aloud, and then have the trios discuss the following questions:

• **What does this verse say about loyalty?**

• **What "adversity" are Ruth and Naomi likely to face as they journey?**

• **What are some hard times you've gone through that left you stronger in the long run?**

• **Can you describe a time when you and a friend grew closer to each other through adversity?**

• **Ruth gave up all that she had to stay with Naomi. Is friendship about giving it all up for someone else? Explain.**

• **What do you have the right to expect from the other person in a friendship?**

Play the clip from *Toy Story 2*, beginning at 1:04:05 when Buzz says, "Woody, you're in danger." End the clip at 1:07:30 when Woody says, "I'm coming with you."

Explain that the movie clip depicts Woody's struggle to overcome his own self-centered attitude and recognize the amazing loyalty of his friends. Prompt students to think about the loyalty Ruth showed to Naomi, even though she knew her life would be terribly hard.

Have teenagers close their eyes and each picture their closest friend. Say: **Think of your friend silently for a moment. What do you appreciate about him or her?** (Pause.) **How have you treated your friend lately? Have you been self-centered or giving?** (Pause.) **We all need encouragement. What have you done to encourage a good friend lately?** (Pause.) **Have you been willing to stick with your friend even during tough times?**

Challenge teenagers to silently brainstorm ways they can encourage their friends, then explain to them that prayer is one of the most powerful ways people can support their friends. Have each student take some time to silently pray for one particular friend—for their friend's needs, spiritual growth, and hurts or frustrations.

After a few moments of silent prayer, wrap this session up by praying aloud that the students will grow in their understanding of friendship over the weekend.

---

small-group discussion 1

Discuss these questions in your small group:

· *Name some groups or cliques in your school who hang out because of similar interests. Is this friendship? Explain.*

· *What is the difference between an acquaintance and a friend?*

· *Share one time a friend has been there for you when life was tough.*

· *Why is it sometimes challenging to be loyal and faithful to a friend?*

---

teaching session 2: heart carving

Before this session, post the various translations of Proverbs 3:3 you've prepared around the room.

Say: **Over the years many different people have translated the Scriptures and,** in an effort to speak to the people of their time, have used different word choices.

Invite several volunteers to read aloud the translations written on the various posters, then ask: • **What does this verse have to do with friendship?**

• **What does it mean to bind these characteristics around our necks?**

Pass out two craft stick halves to each student, and have each teenager select two words from any of the translations of Proverbs 3:3 that he or she thinks is most important in friendship (such as *love*, *faithfulness*, *mercy*, *kindness*, or *truth*). After selecting the two words, the student should write the first letter of each on the end of each craft stick and then, with an adult volunteer's help, should use a hot glue gun to glue the sticks together in the shape of an X. Students can then cut pieces of yarn to tie around their crosses and each create a necklace.

for younger teenagers

If you are not wild about using hot glue guns around junior high students, try this activity using pieces made from card stock or foam core and regular glue.

Gather the students back together, and invite several volunteers to show the others their necklaces and explain why they chose the words they did.

Have students form pairs, and ask: • **When have the words you chose come into play in one of your friendships? Explain.**

• **Has there ever been a time when a friend showed love or faithfulness to you even though you probably didn't deserve it? Describe the situation.**

Say: **In Naomi's time, the worst thing that could happen to a woman was to become a widow. If her husband died, she became the property of his family. Naomi tried to tell her daughters-in-law to go back to their people and find new husbands. Ruth did not go. In fact she had every reason to believe that her life would get worse as a result of this decision.**

Invite a student to read Ruth 1:16 aloud, then say: **Ruth could have gone home. She was young enough that she could have found a new husband and had children. But she made the tough choice to show love, loyalty, mercy, strength, kindness, and truth to Naomi.**

Have pairs discuss these three questions:

• **What would you have done if you were in Ruth's shoes?**

• **Have you ever "walked through fire" for a friend even though you knew you'd probably get burned? What happened?**

• **How is friendship with Jesus similar to the friendship of Ruth and Naomi?**

leader tip

Need game ideas? Check out the game book suggestions on page 7!

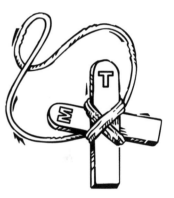

Close by leading the group in prayer, thanking Jesus for being the ultimate friend.

teaching session 3: dear abby

Invite a student to read Ruth 3:1-9 aloud. Ask another volunteer to summarize what the Scripture passage described, then say: **Naomi and Ruth were best friends by this time. Naomi, who was older and wiser, knew she had to find some way for Ruth to find a husband. She instructed Ruth in how to get Boaz's favor.**

Just as with Ruth and Naomi, an important part of friendship is giving and getting advice. Sometimes the advice we get is great, and sometimes it's terrible! Part of being a good friend is knowing when (and when not) to give advice…and also knowing what it means to give the *right* kind of advice.

Have students form eight groups, and give each group one of the slips you prepared from p. 112. (If you have less than sixteen students, have students form pairs and distribute only one of the slips to each pair—it's OK if some are left over.) Instruct groups to read their cards and pretend that the statements represent a close friend asking for advice about a situation. Challenge groups to discuss what they think would be the best advice to give to the friend as well as what they think the worst advice would be. It's OK if group members disagree.

After about five minutes, bring the groups together and ask them to briefly summarize what they discussed.

Ask: • **What role does giving advice play in friendship?**

• **How do you choose who you go to for advice?**

• **What role can your Christian faith play in the advice you give (or don't give) to a friend?**

Say: **Naomi's advice to Ruth may seem strange to us now, but it wasn't at the time. Naomi was a smart woman who knew the system. She knew that as a relative, Boaz would do all he could to care for Ruth.**

Have a student read Ruth 3:10—4:22 aloud, then ask for a volunteer to summarize what happened in the passage. If students are confused, explain that this part of the story contains a complicated process of wheeling and dealing. Boaz has come to love Ruth, so he goes to a "closer kin" and tells him he can buy a field owned by Naomi. He doesn't say, "You have to take Ruth in the bargain," because he knows the kinsman will not want her. He offers the kinsman the land, which of course he accepts. Then he finds out he has to take Ruth in the bargain and he calls the deal off, offering it back to Boaz. So Boaz gets both Ruth and the land. They get married and eventually have a baby named Obed. Explain to teenagers that Obed was the father of Jesse, who was the father of David. And *Jesus* was one of David's descendants.

Say: **Naomi was a good friend—she gave wise advice. Ruth trusted her friend** and did what she advised. In an interesting way, God used their friendship as part of Jesus' own family tree.

Are you a trustworthy friend, faithful and loyal? As a good friend, you can help your friends grow closer to God, and you can help them make wise choices even when it's hard.

---

small-group discussion 2

Discuss these questions in your small group:

· When a friend comes to you with a problem or a tough choice, how do you handle it? Be specific.

· Why do you think Ruth trusted Naomi's advice?

· Have you ever had to give "hard" advice to a friend—advice he or she didn't want to hear? Explain.

· When have you felt ministered to by a friend's advice or encouragement? Explain.

---

teaching session 4: a true friend

Begin by asking the group to shout out things they know about Jesus, and write the responses on a dry-erase board.

Ask: • **Imagine you were one of Jesus' close friends, like Mary, Martha, or Lazarus. What kind of friend would Jesus be?**

Write the responses on the board.

Prompt students to form trios and read John 15:15 in their groups. Invite the trios to discuss the following questions:

• **How does it make you feel to know that God wants to be your friend?**

• **How is friendship with Jesus similar to relationships with human friends?**

• **How is it different?**

Say: **A long, long time ago, friends would communicate by writing letters on parchment and having someone walk miles and miles (or perhaps ride a horse) to deliver the letter. Today, communication with friends is a lot different! We have the telephone, the postal service, e-mail, instant messaging, and Internet chats.**

Did you know that God wants to communicate with you in the same way you

communicate with your friends? He wants to hear what's going on in your life—and he wants you to get to know him better too!

Pass out copies of the "Instant Message" handout (p. 113) to students along with pencils or pens. Explain that human friendships are great, but the most awesome friendship we can ever have is with God. Instruct students to spread out and each spend some time alone filling out the "Instant Message" sheet to represent a prayer conversation between them and God. Tell them to be honest and to use this exercise as a chance to get to know Jesus better as a friend.

Encourage students to write as much as they want to. When everyone has "signed off," gather them together and talk about what the experience was like. Those who want to share parts of their conversations may do so.

Explain to the students that Jesus is *always* with them—they can always "Instant Message" him about anything. Pass out the hole-punched index cards (one for each student), and challenge each teenager to write down three words that represent three different ways they are thankful to God for his friendship. Encourage them to keep their cards for the worship session.

worship session: strong branches

If you can hold this worship session outside, find a tree with low branches and gather around it. If you are stuck inside due to weather, set up an artificial tree and have the group stand around it.

Say: **Let's take another look at what Ruth says to Naomi.**

Read Ruth 1:16-17 aloud and ask: • **Is this something you could say to Jesus? Is it something Jesus has already said to you?**

• **Is this something you could say to another person? Why or why not? Under what circumstances?**

Ask teenagers to spend a few minutes quietly thinking about all they have learned and discussed over the weekend. How do they each want to grow as a friend? How can they improve their relationships with others? With God? Encourage students to write down, on the blank side of their index cards, three ways that they want to apply what they've learned. When they've finished writing, pass out the pieces of yarn and have them each loop their piece of yarn through the hole of their cards.

Say: **Trees are a lot like relationships. Some of them can take a lot of abuse or weight. Others cannot. If you look at pictures on the news after a huge storm, you see that sometimes even giant trees get blown over. It's the trees that are stiff that crack under the pressure.**

Friendships are that way. Some trees can weather the storms because they can bend. They can be flexible. Trees will survive a storm because they can twist and

turn. If our friendships are to survive the challenges of life, we must do the same.

This is also true of our relationship with God. God is our friend. He won't solve all our problems for us, but he will help hold us up in the storm. He will ride it out with us. He will be there beside us. He will help us carry the weight. There is nothing we can do to separate ourselves from God's love.

Encourage students to spend some time praying about the things they've written on both sides of their cards. They should finish their prayers by tying their cards to the various branches of the tree.

Signs

Take a look at the signs you see along the highway, and consider how they symbolize different aspects of friendship. Follow the example and write your thoughts by each sign.

 You may not always get your own way in a friendship. Sometimes friendship is about giving others the right of way to pursue their own ideas.

Think of a close friend. Which road sign most accurately describes your relationship?

Read 1 Corinthians 13:4-7. In the space below, create your own "sign" that signifies an important quality of friendship.

Student Quiet Time 2: Circle of Friends

Make a list of six people on the back of this page: three good friends, your parents (or two family members), and God. Write your name in the circle below. Now draw a circle for each of the names you just listed. Here's the idea: The space between your circle and the others should represent the "space" between you and that person in real life. Your closest friend will be closer to you on the page. Someone you don't feel close to will be farther away. You can overlap the circles if you want to. No one will see this but you, so be honest.

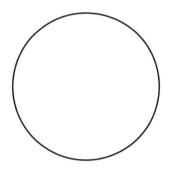

Take a look at your drawing. What does this say about the relationships you have? Who is the farthest from you? What keeps them so far away? What does the person closest to you have that you don't have with the other circles?

Write down three things you can do in the next month to shorten the distance between you and your farthest circle.

Read James 2:23. Are you God's friend? How can your friendship with God grow?

Dear Abby

Instructions: Photocopy this page and cut out the cards along the dotted lines.

I really want to ask a certain girl (or guy) out. Should I do it? How should I do it?

I'm having a really hard time deciding which college to go to. Any advice?

I want to take a year off after high school and do mission work in another country, but I'm afraid my parents will totally freak out. What should I do?

I've been invited to a great party for this weekend, but I'm pretty sure there will be drinking there. Is it a big deal if I go?

I've been flirting with a guy (or girl) in an Internet chat room. He (or she) wants my number…should I give it to him (or her)?

I got in a car accident last weekend—I was goofing around and crashed the car. My parents are really ticked at me. What should I do?

I'm really starting to have doubts about my faith in God. I don't even know if God really exists. Any advice?

I caught somebody looking at my math test and copying my answers. It makes me really mad, but I don't want to cause problems. What should I do?

INSTANT MESSAGE

Imagine it is Sunday evening. You are finishing up tomorrow's homework when you hear a familiar sound and an instant message appears on your computer screen. You think it's from a friend but then realize this one is different—it's from Jesus.

Fill in your personal screen name in the blanks, and then keep the conversation going as long as you want. You can have extra paper. Think about how Jesus would respond based on all the things you've talked about during this retreat.

G-zuz: Are you there?

_____: Who is this?

G-zuz: Read the screen name.

_____: You're Jesus?

G-zuz: Yep.

_____: Why are you writing to me?

G-zuz: Because you are my friend. Tell me what's going on in your life…

_____:

G-zuz:

_____:

G-zuz:

_____:

G-zuz:

_____:

G-zuz:

(Keep the conversation going. Write on the back if you need to.)

master supply list

In addition to basic retreat supplies such as food, games, Bibles, pens, pencils, paper, and worship music, you'll also need the following supplies:

- ❏ 1 masquerade costume mask for each student (available at craft stores)
- ❏ flip chart
- ❏ markers
- ❏ craft supplies such as craft glue, sequins, feathers, glitter, paints, and felt
- ❏ 1 photocopy of "Student Quiet Time 1: Say Thank You!" (p. 123) for each student
- ❏ 1 photocopy of "Small-Group Discussion 1" box (p. 118) for each small group
- ❏ several recent newspapers containing stories on current events
- ❏ several blindfolds
- ❏ several pairs of earplugs
- ❏ matches
- ❏ wood
- ❏ charcoal grill or fire pit
- ❏ basin
- ❏ water
- ❏ soap
- ❏ towels
- ❏ 1 index card for each student
- ❏ 1 photocopy of "Small-Group Discussion 2" box (p. 121) for each small group
- ❏ 1 photocopy of "Student Quiet Time 2: A Real-Life Story" (p. 124)
- ❏ several skeins of embroidery floss in various colors
- ❏ 1 safety pin for each student
- ❏ scissors
- ❏ several photocopies of "Wristband Instructions" handout (p. 125)

rugged prayer

retreat focus: Through studying David and the psalms, students will learn that true intimacy with God can be found in honest transparent communication with their Creator.

retreat motto: Worship without pretending.

theme verse: "O Lord, you have searched me and you know me" (Psalm 139:1).

preparation

Before the retreat, gather all of the necessary supplies and make all of the photocopies recommended in the Master Supply List.

For Small-Group Discussion 2, prepare a set of index cards for each small group by writing different emotions on the cards in each set, such as anger, joy, jealousy, despair, happiness, depression, peacefulness, delight, surprise, wonder, or sorrow.

For Teaching Session 4, follow the "Wristband Instructions" (p. 125) to create a sample wristband.

Make sure students are divided into small groups (for more information on this, see p. 7), and take some time to study the life of David in 1 Samuel; 2 Samuel; 1 Kings 1–2; and Psalms 13; 51; 54; 103; and 139.

worship idea

For your theme song for the weekend, use "The Heart of Worship" from the two-CD set *I Could Sing of Your Love Forever*. For information on ordering student lyrics books, a song leader book, and the CDs, call Group at 1-800-447-1070.

suggested schedule

2-Night Retreat

Day	Time	Activity	Supplies
Friday	6:00-7:00 p.m.	Games	
	7:00-8:30 p.m.	Teaching Session 1: The Real David	Bibles, flip chart, markers, pens, paper, masquerade masks, art supplies
	8:30-9:30 p.m.	Free Time	
	9:30-10:00 p.m.	Small-Group Discussion 1	Photocopies of "Small-Group Discussion 1" box (p. 118)
	10:00-10:30 p.m.	Snacks	
	11:00 p.m.	Lights Out	
Saturday	7:30-8:00 a.m.	Student Quiet Time 1: Say Thank You!	Bibles, photocopies of "Student Quiet Time 1: Say Thank You!" (p. 124), pencils or pens
	8:00-9:00 a.m.	Breakfast	
	9:00-10:00 a.m.	Games or Group Activities	
	10:00-11:30 a.m.	Teaching Session 2: A Song of Despair	Bibles, paper, pencils or pens, newspapers
	11:30 a.m.-12:30 p.m.	Lunch	
	12:30-6:00 p.m.	Free Time or Group Activities	
	6:00-7:00 p.m.	Dinner	
	7:00-8:30 p.m.	Teaching Session 3: Get Right With God	Bibles, blindfolds, earplugs, paper, pencils or pens, wood, matches, grill or fire pit, bowl of water, soap, towels
	8:30-9:30 p.m.	Free Time	
	9:30-10:00 p.m.	Small-Group Discussion 2	Index cards with emotions written on them, photocopies of "Small-Group Discussion 2" box (p. 121)
	10:00-10:30 p.m.	Snacks	
	11:00 p.m.	Lights Out	
Sunday	7:30-8:00 a.m.	Student Quiet Time 2: A Real-Life Story	Bibles, photocopies of "Student Quiet Time 2: A Real-Life Story" (p. 124), pencils or pens
	8:00-9:00 a.m.	Breakfast	
	9:00-10:30 a.m.	Teaching Session 4: Confidence to Be Real	Bibles, skeins of embroidery floss, scissors, safety pins, photocopies of "Wristband Instructions" handout (p. 125), sample wristband
	10:30 a.m.-noon	Games or Group Activities	

Day	Time	Activity	Supplies
Friday	6:00-7:00 p.m.	Games	
	7:00-8:30 p.m.	Teaching Session 1: The Real David	Bibles, flip chart, markers, pens, paper, masquerade masks, art supplies
	8:30-9:30 p.m.	Free Time	
	9:30-10:00 p.m.	Small-Group Discussion 1	Photocopies of "Small-Group Discussion 1" box (p. 118)
	10:00-10:30 p.m.	Snacks	
	11:00 p.m.	Lights Out	
Saturday	7:30-8:00 a.m.	Student Quiet Time 1: Say Thank You!	Bibles, photocopies of "Student Quiet Time 1: Say Thank You!" (p. 123), pencils or pens
	8:00-9:00 a.m.	Breakfast	
	9:00-9:30 a.m.	Small-Group Discussion 2	Index cards with emotions written on them, photocopies of "Small-Group Discussion 2" box (p. 121)
	9:30-10:30 a.m.	Games or Group Activities	
	10:30 a.m.-noon	Teaching Session 4: Confidence to Be Real	Bibles, skeins of embroidery floss, scissors, safety pins, photocopies of "Wristband Instructions" handout (p. 125), sample wristband

teaching session 1: the real david

Ask the students to shout out what they already know about David, and use a flip chart to write the facts they know as a timeline of his life. Make sure to include the following events in your list:

- Saul is made the first king of Israel. He displeases God.

- Samuel the prophet anoints David as the next king while Saul is still alive.

- David kills Goliath.

- David works for Saul; he becomes good friends with Jonathan, Saul's son.

- Saul tries to kill David.

- David goes on the run, and he becomes a mighty warrior.

- Saul and Jonathan are killed.

- David becomes king.

Split the students into four groups—you should have a maximum of eight students in each group, so if there are more students, form more than four groups and repeat some of the Bible passage assignments. Assign each group one of the following Bible passages: 1 Samuel 17:1-54; 1 Samuel 19:1-18 and 21:10–22:2; 2 Samuel 11:1–12:22; and 2 Samuel 6:1-23. Explain that they should use the passage to try to develop an idea of what David was like, trying to get inside his character. They can use these questions to help them:

- **What was David feeling in this passage?**

leader tip

You may want to begin each teaching session with five to ten minutes of singing. In addition to the suggested theme song, select other praise and worship songs that will complement the theme of the weekend.

• **How would he have appeared to other people? Would it be different from how he might have *felt*?**

• **What words would you use to describe his character? What type of a person was he?**

Each group should then prepare a "catwalk" show of the David they have discovered in their passage. In fashion shows, models stroll down a catwalk while an emcee describes the clothes that they are wearing. The group should choose one student to act the part of David, walking up and down in an appropriate way, while another student plays the part of the emcee, describing David's character (not his clothes!) and how he appeared. Other members of the group could hum a suitable theme song or play the part of other characters. Each group should aim to communicate its assigned story. Encourage students to be creative!

Enjoy the catwalk shows! Afterward, discuss the different representations of David. Ask:

• **Were there any aspects of David's character that came across in all four situations?**

• **Having studied one part of David's life, were you surprised to see how different David was in other situations?**

• **What emotions have you seen David go through in these four representations?**

Say: **People would have seen many different things when they looked at David: shepherd boy, warrior, musician, husband, king, adulterer. Similarly, people looking at us will see different things. What kind of an image do we portray? What words would other people use to describe us? How much of the "real us" is visible? How much do we want to keep hidden? What kind of masks do we wear?**

Explain that students are going to learn how others see them. Use tape to stick a piece of paper to each student's back. Students should then mingle and write on one another's pieces of paper words that describe the way they view one another. These should all be phrased positively—there should be no nasty surprises!

After about ten minutes, students should take off these pieces of paper and read them. Talk about them if that seems appropriate—are there any surprises? Next, hand out masquerade masks and art supplies. Give students some time to make masks that represent how they appear to others. They can use the words on their sheets of paper, as well as other ideas of their own.

Take some time to look at the finished masks. Then ask students to quietly reflect on how true to themselves these masks are. How much do they portray the real person behind the mask? Are there things that they keep hidden from others?

Ask students to write inside their masks some of the things they keep hidden from

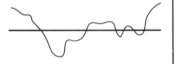

others…and why. Tell them that they don't need to show what they've written to anyone else unless they choose to, so they can be as honest as they like.

for younger teenagers

Younger teenagers may never have thought before about how others see them. Allow them to write words on the outside of their masks if they find that easier than decorating their masks.

Finish the session by explaining the main focus of this retreat. Say: **Often Christians think they should always be leading a triumphant life—that expressing pain or doubt or negative feelings can feel like failure, or a lack of faith. So we hide behind masks, afraid to show other people what we are really like. And yet in the psalms we find honesty in the words addressed to God—despair, cries for help, joyous praise, doubt, faith, pain, and laughter. God doesn't want us to pretend or to hide behind masks—he wants us to be honest in our prayers and in our worship.**

---

small-group discussion 1

Discuss these questions in your small group:

· Share a secret that no one else knows about you—it could be a happy secret, a funny one, or a sad one.

· Are there some things about you that you never ever want to tell anyone? What sort of things do we keep hidden from one another? Why?

· How do you feel about the fact that God knows all about you?

· What do those feelings say about your understanding of who God is and what God is like?

---

teaching session 2: a song of despair

Hand out pieces of paper and pens to everyone, and explain that you want them to think back over the last week and draw a chart of their experiences. They should draw a line horizontally across the middle of the page, then think back over the highs and lows of the last week and draw them on the chart—positive experiences and feelings above the line and negative experiences and feelings below the line. Compare the charts. Who has had the best week? Who has had the most zigzag week with the most ups and downs?

Ask: • **Where was God through all these experiences? How do you know? Were you aware of his presence?**

• **What words describe the positive feelings you had?** (Ask everyone to name at least one feeling.)

• **How could you have expressed those feelings in worship? What songs, Bible passages, or prayers could you have used?**

• **What words describe the negative feelings you had?** (Again, ask everyone to name at least one.)

• **How could those feelings have been expressed in worship? What appropriate songs, Bible passages, and prayers do you know?**

Say: **We don't often sing worship songs of despair, fear, or depression. Most of our worship songs are full of faith and praise, which is great, but sometimes we may feel that we can't bring negative feelings to God—that somehow we should pretend to be happy all the time in his presence. But God was with you through all the ups *and* downs of the last week. We don't need to be afraid to express all our feelings to him.**

Have someone read Psalm 13:1-6 to the group while everyone else reads along in their Bibles. Ask: • **Has anyone read this psalm before? Are you surprised that it is in the Bible?**

• **David is being really honest about how he feels. What stops us from being honest in church about how we feel?**

• **Would it work to sing a song like this during a worship time in church? Why or why not?**

Give students a few minutes to write their own psalms of lament and despair. They can look at their charts of the last week and remember how they felt in one of the low times, or they can look through newspaper articles about current events to find things that make them sad or discouraged, then write short psalms expressing their feelings. Say: **Psalms don't have to rhyme or be in poetic language. They should be heartfelt and honest—just what you want to say to God.**

Ask one of the students to read aloud verses 5 and 6 of Psalm 13 again. Say: **This psalm has a very important "but..." in it.**

Ask: • **Do these last verses contradict the rest of the psalm? Has David suddenly changed his mind?**

• **Is it possible to have faith in the midst of doubt? How might David have said these verses aloud?**

Say: **It's important to affirm faith in the midst of despair, to have hope that God will change things, even if you don't know how that will happen.** Ask students to go back to their psalms of despair and add their own affirmations of hope at the end of their psalms. This needs to be real for them—something they are sure of, even in the midst of despair.

leader tip

To preserve students' integrity, you shouldn't try to make them write psalms of lament and despair if they don't feel that way! If looking at news stories or the events of the last week doesn't arouse feelings of sorrow, then let them write psalms expressing more positive feelings instead. Affirm their experience, and ask them to share their psalms at a mealtime or in a worship time rather than in this session.

Conclude by asking a few students to read their psalms aloud.

teaching session 3: get right with god

Ask students to form pairs and begin talking about their earliest memories (or any other easy-to-talk-about topic). Allow them to talk for a few minutes, and then introduce an obstacle to the conversation—they have to move six feet apart. Get them talking again, and then gradually introduce these other hindrances: One person is blindfolded, then the other has to speak with a finger on his or her mouth, then one person has to wear earplugs. Encourage them to keep talking! After a few minutes, remove all the hindrances and let them talk for a bit longer.

Then bring everyone back together and ask: • **What was it like having to hold a conversation with those restrictions? How did you feel?**

• **If those obstacles remained in place for a long time, how do you think it would affect your relationship with the other person?**

• **What was it like to be able to talk freely again?**

Say: **This symbolizes what happens to our relationship with God when we sin. God still loves us and wants to keep talking to us, but our sin gets in the way, spoiling the communication, causing distance between God and us.**

Remind students of one of the episodes in David's life that you looked at in the first session—his adultery with Bathsheba, his murder of Uriah, and the death of his son. This was pretty serious sin; David was confronted by Nathan and had to face up to what he had done.

Ask one person to read Psalm 51 aloud, and make sure everyone else reads along in their Bibles. Ask: • **What are the ways that David asks for forgiveness? Pick out the different things that he asks God to do.**

• **Does David give excuses or reasons for what he has done? Explain.**

• **Does David expect forgiveness? What aspects of God's character does he appeal to?**

Say: **This is a beautiful prayer of confession and repentance. Although we haven't done the same things that David did, we still need to confess our sin to God, asking for his forgiveness and reminding ourselves of his unfailing love.**

Give students time on their own to think about anything that they need to confess to God. If they want to, they could write these sins on paper, or draw symbols that represent the things they have done wrong.

Prepare a small fire outside in a fire pit or charcoal grill. Gather students around and read aloud Psalm 51 once more. One by one, invite them to throw their pieces of paper on the fire, allowing them to burn as symbols of their repentance. Have some warm water,

leader tip

Need game ideas? Check out the game book suggestions on page 7!

leader tip

Remind students that they don't need to rake around to find sins or feel like they have to make something up. They should ask the Holy Spirit to show them where their relationship with God is spoiled by sin and then spend some time quietly listening for the answer.

soap, and towels nearby. Students could then wash their hands to symbolize God washing them clean. End with a song of worship to enable students to express their thanks to God for his forgiveness. Stress that they are forgiven, washed clean—those sins are gone and so are the barriers in their relationship to God. That's cause for celebration!

small-group discussion 2

(Instructions: Get a set of index cards from your youth leader before this discussion.)

Take turns drawing index cards and then answering these questions:

• When did you last feel the emotion written on this card? Tell us about what happened.

• Has God ever felt that emotion? Can anyone in the group think of a Bible story or a situation where God might express that emotion?

After everyone has picked a card, discuss:

• What difference does it make to know that God has felt these things too? How does it help your understanding of God and your relationship with him?

teaching session 4: confidence to be real

Have students bring along their masks and any psalms they have written, so that there is a sense of bringing together all that they have experienced to this concluding session.

Start with a few rounds of the well-known "trust-fall" game, where a volunteer falls backward into someone's arms. Do this by having the group form a close circle around a volunteer who falls back against someone's arms and is then pushed gently back into a standing position in the center of the circle. As trust is built up among the students, volunteers can be allowed to fall farther or be pushed back more energetically.

Debrief students about this experience by asking:

• What was it like for the first person to try this activity? How did you feel? Were you afraid? What helped your confidence grow?

• For those who volunteered later, did it help that you had seen what had happened already? Would you have wanted to go first?

• What was the experience of the group providing the support? Did you like being trusted? Were you tempted to break that trust and let the person fall?

Say: **Having confidence in the people around us enables us to relax and be** ourselves. **We have talked a lot this weekend about being real with God in worship and prayer, about not being afraid to express how we feel, about not having to pretend in God's presence. We need to know that we can trust God with our real selves.**

Have the students lie down or sit comfortably and close their eyes while someone reads Psalm 139:1-18, 23-24 to them. Encourage the students to use their imaginations to enter into what this psalm is saying. Then allow them some time to read the text themselves, taking ownership of the words, and thanking God that he made them and loves them.

Say: **Knowing that God created us, that he knows us inside and out, that he will always be with us, gives us the courage and confidence to be ourselves in his presence.**

Explain that you will finish this retreat with a worship experience. Students will make wristbands with different colored threads, following the instruction sheet (p. 125). The different colors can represent the different emotions and experiences of our lives that can all be woven together and brought to God who is always with us. While they work to make their wristbands, students should discuss with their friends what the different colors represent and why they have chosen them. At the end, invite them to tie on their wristbands as you pray for them to continue to be real in God's presence, bringing every part of their lives in worship to him.

STUDENT QUIET TIME 1:
Say Thank You!

Read Psalm 103:1-22. David is almost telling himself to be thankful: "Praise the Lord, O my soul." Maybe he wasn't feeling great, but he found plenty to praise God for. How thankful to God do you feel? Whether it comes naturally or not, this morning you are going to wake up your soul by praising! Write down three things from the psalm that you also want to praise God for:

Think about the things God has done for you in the past—maybe answers to prayer...or freedom from fear. Write down your thanks here:

Think about God's promises to you for the future. What difference does it make knowing that God will provide for you? Include those praises, too.

And what about all the things that we often take for granted—food, water, a place to live? Don't forget to thank God for these!

Stand up and read through your praise to God, out loud if you are alone! You may want to craft these ideas into your own psalm of praise. Try to stay thankful throughout the day, continually bringing your thanks and praise to God.

Student Quiet Time 2:
A REAL-LiFE STORY

Some of the psalms in the Bible can be linked to specific events in David's life. It's fascinating to read the events that led to those psalms; it gives us insight into how David must have been feeling.

Read about these background events of Psalm 54: David is on the run from Saul, who is threatening to kill him. David has lots of warriors with him and they keep having to move from place to place to escape Saul. And then David is betrayed...Read 1 Samuel 23:13-23. How do you think David might have felt? What would he say to God?

Now read the psalm that he wrote: Psalm 54. Read it through a few times—imagine how David must have felt to have his life put in danger.

Choose an event in your life that could inspire a psalm. It could be something happy, or sad, or scary...

Spend some time remembering the event. How did you feel? What did you want God to do for you? David ends Psalm 54 stating his faith in God in spite of the difficulties he faces. How could you end your psalm? Write it out here:

Wristband Instructions

Supplies: 4 different colored strands of embroidery floss (each strand about 2 feet long) and 1 safety pin for each person.

How to Make a Wristband

1. Knot the strands together, about 3 inches from the end. Pin the knot to your pants just above the knee and take a seat. Spread the strands out and mentally number them from 1 to 4, starting at the left.

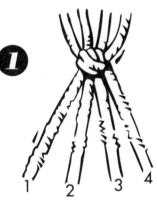

2. Hold strand number 2 taut with your left hand and knot strand number 1 around it, as indicated in the picture. Pull strand 1 upward until it is tightly knotted around strand 2.

3. Move strand 2 over to the left—you have finished with this strand for the time being. Now hold strand 3 taut with your left hand. Knot strand 1 around it in the same way as you did around strand 2.

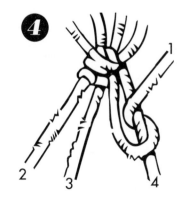

4. Move strand 3 over to the left. Hold strand 4 taut with your left hand and knot strand 1 around it.

You have just completed the first row of the wristband by moving strand 1 from left to right and knotting it around each of the strands. Now mentally renumber the strands from 1 to 4, starting at the left, and begin again.

Simply measure the wristband as you go, and stop tying knots when it reaches the length you'd like. Tie a knot at the end, and tie the band around your wrist.

standing strong, hanging on

master supply list

In addition to basic retreat supplies such as food, games, Bibles, pens, pencils, paper, and worship music, you'll also need the following supplies:

- ❑ 15 sheets of newsprint (or pieces of poster board)
- ❑ 1 large index card for each student
- ❑ markers
- ❑ *I Could Sing of Your Love Forever* CD (or another CD which contains the song "Shout to the Lord")
- ❑ CD player
- ❑ 1 photocopy of "Small-Group Discussion 1" box (p. 130) for each small group
- ❑ 1 photocopy of "Student Quiet Time 1: Imprisoned" (p. 135) for each student
- ❑ house key
- ❑ hand mirror
- ❑ a few coins
- ❑ blanket
- ❑ box of crayons
- ❑ box of facial tissue
- ❑ ring (costume jewelry, plain band, or plastic jewelry is best)
- ❑ puzzle piece
- ❑ 1 photocopy of "Practice Makes Perfect" handout (p. 139)
- ❑ 2 empty plastic 2-liter bottles
- ❑ large candle
- ❑ matches
- ❑ wrapped gift box
- ❑ 1 gift tag for each student
- ❑ 1 photocopy of "Spiritual Willpower" handout (pp. 137-138)
- ❑ stepladder or table

(continued on p. 128)

retreat focus: Students will investigate what it means to hold on to faith when life is hard by studying the amazing example of Joseph.

retreat motto: Forever I'll stand.

theme verse: "Look to the Lord and his strength; seek his face always" (Psalm 105:4).

preparation

Before the retreat, gather all of the necessary supplies and make all of the photocopies recommended in the Master Supply List.

For Teaching Session 1, write the following words or phrases on separate sheets of newsprint: family problems, jealousy, victimization, greed, isolation, lies, grief, disloyalty, questioning God, misunderstanding, resentment.

For Teaching Session 2, create three more newsprint posters with the following words on them: humility, joy, gifts.

For Teaching Session 3, cut apart the slips on the "Practice Makes Perfect" handout (p. 139), fold them, and put them in a paper bag. (If you have more than twenty-two students, create more slips of paper with statements that could be really difficult for someone to deal with.)

For Teaching Session 4, put approximately one handful of sand into each resealable plastic bag and seal the bags; you should have one bag of sand for each student.

Make sure students are divided into small groups (for more information on this, see p. 7), and take some time to study Genesis 37 and 39–50 on your own.

worship idea

For your theme song for the weekend, use "Shout to the Lord" from the two-CD set *I Could Sing of Your Love Forever.* For information on ordering the student lyrics books, a song leader book, and the CDs, call Group at 1-800-447-1070.

suggested schedule

2-Night Retreat

Day	Time	Activity	Supplies
Friday	6:00-7:00 p.m.	Games	
	7:00-8:00 p.m.	Teaching Session 1: The Power to Persist	Bibles, newsprint posters, tape, markers, CD player, *I Could Sing of Your Love Forever* CDs, large index cards
	8:00-9:30 p.m.	Games or Group Activities	
	9:30-10:00 p.m.	Small-Group Discussion 1	Photocopies of "Small-Group Discussion 1" box (p. 130)
	10:00-10:30 p.m.	Snacks	
	11:00 p.m.	Lights Out	
Saturday	7:30-8:00 a.m.	Student Quiet Time 1: Imprisoned	Bibles, photocopies of "Student Quiet Time 1: Imprisoned" (p. 135), pencils or pens
	8:00-9:00 a.m.	Breakfast	
	9:00-10:30 a.m.	Free Time or Group Activities	
	10:30 a.m.-noon	Teaching Session 2: Be Prepared	Bibles, newsprint, markers, house key, mirror, coins, blanket, crayons, paper, facial tissue, ring, puzzle piece, bottle, candle and matches, wrapped gift box, gift tags, photocopy of "Spiritual Willpower" handout (pp. 137-138), two chairs, stepladder or table, throw rug, large bowl, dry cereal
	noon-1:00 p.m.	Lunch	
	1:00-5:00 p.m.	Free Time or Group Activities	
	5:00-6:30 p.m.	Teaching Session 3: Practice Makes Perfect	Bibles, photocopy of "Practice Makes Perfect" handout (p. 139), paper, pens, paper bag, flashlights
	6:30-7:30 p.m.	Dinner	
	7:30-8:00 p.m.	Small-Group Discussion 2	Photocopies of "Small-Group Discussion 2" box (p. 133)
	8:00-10:00 p.m.	Games or Group Activities	
	10:00-10:30 p.m.	Snacks	
	11:00 p.m.	Lights Out	
Sunday	7:30-8:00 a.m.	Student Quiet Time 2: God on My Mind	Bibles, photocopies of "Student Quiet Time 2: God on My Mind" (p. 136), pencils or pens
	8:00-9:00 a.m.	Breakfast	
	9:00-10:00 a.m.	Games or Group Activities	
	10:00-11:00 a.m.	Teaching Session 4: Prop It Up With Prayer, Baby!	Bibles, resealable bags, one large bottle, bags of sand
	11:00 a.m.-noon	Free Time	

Day	Time	Activity	Supplies
Friday	6:00-7:00 p.m.	Games	
	7:00-8:00 p.m.	Teaching Session 1: The Power to Persist	Bibles, newsprint posters, tape, markers, CD player, *I Could Sing of Your Love Forever* CDs, large index cards
	8:00-9:30 p.m.	Free Time	
	9:30-10:00 p.m.	Small-Group Discussion 1	Photocopies of "Small-Group Discussion 1" box (p. 130)
	10:00-10:30 p.m.	Snacks	
	11:00 p.m.	Lights Out	
Saturday	7:30-8:00 a.m.	Student Quiet Time 1: Imprisoned	Bibles, photocopies of "Student Quiet Time 1: Imprisoned" (p. 135), pencils or pens
	8:00-9:00 a.m.	Breakfast	
	9:00-10:30 a.m.	Games or Group Activities	
	10:30 a.m.-noon	Teaching Session 3: Practice Makes Perfect	Bibles, photocopy of "Practice Makes Perfect" handout (p. 139), paper, pens, paper bag, flashlights

(continued from p. 126)

❑ throw rug
❑ large bowl
❑ dry cereal
❑ paper bag
❑ several flashlights
❑ 1 photocopy of "Small-Group Discussion 2" box (p. 133) for each small group
❑ 1 photocopy of "Student Quiet Time 2: God on My Mind" (p. 136) for each student
❑ 1 resealable plastic bag for each student
❑ sand (enough for a handful of sand for each student)

teaching session 1: the power to persist

Tape the newsprint posters you prepared in various places throughout the room, and leave them up for the rest of the retreat. Gather the students together and hand each student a large index card and a marker. Ask them to sit and take a minute to read through the posters.

Say: **The theme verse for this weekend is, "Look to the Lord and his strength; seek his face always" from Psalm 105:4. That seems pretty simple: Always seek his face. Stand forever in your faith. It may be simple, but the tricky part here is in the word *always*. During the tough times in our lives, it can be difficult to seek God's face always. We're focusing this retreat on those tough times, when our spiritual life is challenged. After this weekend, you will know the skills that help you in your challenge to "stand forever" in your faith. You will learn how faith can be strengthened when you persist, prepare, practice, and pray. And we'll use the biblical stories surrounding the life of Joseph to help us better understand the way faith can survive life's struggles.**

Your first step is to strengthen your power to persist. Two challenges I give you tonight will help you hone your skills of persistence.

For the first challenge, tell students that one important part of persisting is knowing and growing in God's love. Give them ten minutes to each find something that represents his or her love for God. For example, students might return with a Bible (God's Word reminds me of how much he loves me), water (God's love refreshes and replenishes me), a rock (God's love is my strength), a favorite shirt (God's love is comfortable and fits me well), a blade of grass (God's creation is a gift of love), or a blank piece of paper (I don't know how God feels about me).

When everyone has returned with their items, gather them together and ask some students to share the meaning of their objects. Then ask these questions:

- **Was it difficult to find something that represented God's love? Why or why not?**

- **How does God's love reflect your relationship with him?**

Say: **Your first "persistence" challenge starting tonight is to keep the item you've chosen with you at all times throughout the weekend. Keep track of when it's difficult to carry this item around and, if you decide to stop carrying it, why you stopped. Remember, part of "seeking God's face always" is holding on to your love for him. Now let's spend a little time in worship.**

Ask students to sit down, take a look at the posters you've put up around the room, and each identify one that exemplifies a tough time in their lives. Ask them to write the word or phrase on their index cards. Wait a few moments in silence as students reflect on their words.

Say: **As you learn more about the life of Joseph, you'll see him as an example of spiritual strength. No matter what happened in Joseph's life, God was always with him. Joseph's love for God and obedience to him persisted.**

Tell kids to turn over their index cards as you play "Shout to the Lord" (from the *I Could Sing of Your Love Forever* two-CD set) and each write on the back of the card a word or phrase from the song that resonates with them, something that can remind them of God's strength during tough times.

When you've played through the song once and everyone has chosen a word, ask teenagers to hold up their index cards with the words from the posters facing out. As you play the song a second time, tell the students that when they hear the word or phrase they chose from the song, they'll stand up, flip their index cards over to reveal those words, and remain standing for the rest of the song.

After the song is over, ask the students to remain standing.

Say: **Tonight, your second challenge is to remain standing—to remain on your feet for the rest of the evening. While you're eating, while you're talking, while you're...OK, bathroom breaks can be an exception. Keep in mind that you don't *have* to stand all evening. Whether you follow through with this challenge is completely your decision. But let's read a little about Joseph's challenges and see how he was able to persist, to stand strong.**

Separate the students into two groups—have one read Genesis 37:12-36 and the other read Genesis 39:1-19. Then ask groups to discuss this question:

- **If you were Joseph, do you think your faith could stand through this difficult time? Why or why not?**

Invite the groups to come back together and summarize their readings and discussions. Close by praying that the students will have the strength of Joseph to remain

leader tip

You may want to begin each teaching session with five to ten minutes of singing. In addition to the suggested theme song, select other praise and worship songs that will complement the theme of the weekend.

leader tip

If you have students with special needs or with an inability to stand, simply change the challenge of standing to something else. Your challenge could be as simple as remaining quiet or holding a bowl of candy without eating it. Or you can create several challenges and allow students to choose one.

"standing" with God through any challenges. Ask students to each read at least one chapter of Genesis 37–45 sometime before the teaching session tomorrow. You may want to assign specific chapters to students so that all chapters can be summarized before the activity in tomorrow's session.

small-group discussion 1

Discuss these questions in your small group:

· Is it difficult to stand all this time? Why or why not?

· How is the challenge to stand like your challenge to stand forever with God, to seek his face always?

· What kinds of techniques can you use to give you the "power to persist" with your faith and eliminate the "reasons to resist" your faith?

teaching session 2: be prepared

Before this session, go to the room where you've hung the posters with words on them. Use the "Spiritual Willpower" handout (pp. 137-138) to write Scriptures and questions beneath the word on each poster. Write the instructions from the handout for each poster as well. Place the designated item for each word beneath each poster. In the center of the room, place a large candle on the sheet of newsprint with the word *Joy* written on it, and light the candle. Around it place two chairs (one facing toward it and one away), a stepladder or sturdy table, and a throw rug (place the rug a little farther away from the candle). Also hang the "humility" and "gifts" posters and follow instructions for those stations. Leave one station empty—just a blank piece of newsprint and a marker, for students to write their own emotion or Scripture.

Begin the session by asking students to summarize the chapters of Genesis 37–45. Add any important events that they've left out.

Say: **We've learned a lot about persistence. But sometimes you can be caught off guard by a tough situation, and you never are able to gain that willpower to strengthen your faith. Emotional trauma, shock, or denial can all cause someone to walk away from God, unless the person prepares for those times and practices relying on faith to pull through. That's what we'll do today. Our P word this morning is** *prepare,* **and by looking at how we've handled situations in the past, we can see how they've affected our relationship with God now—or how they** *could* **have affected it.**

Tell students to each take a turn walking through the stations you set up earlier, thinking specifically about a tough situation they've had to deal with in the past or are currently struggling with. They should go to each station that lists a word or emotion that is part of their own tough situation and follow the instructions. Ask them to take Bibles with them. If they have experienced any feelings not listed, they can advance to the "blank" station and write the feelings they had.

Allow eight to ten students at a time to walk through the stations. As they leave the room, allow other students to enter it, making sure no more than ten people are in the room at the same time. Have the rest of the students sit around a bowl full of dry cereal and munch on it as they read Genesis 41:15-49. Students waiting to go through the stations should discuss these questions as they eat some cereal:

• **How did Joseph prepare for the coming famine?**

• **If this bowl of cereal was all you had to eat for the next week, how would you treat it differently?**

• **How are Joseph's dreams like your own communication with God?**

• **How can planning for upcoming events strengthen your relationship with God?**

After everyone has walked through the "Spiritual Willpower" path, have the entire group discuss these questions:

• **As you "walked through" your tough situation, did you determine that the situation brought you closer to God or moved you further away from him? Explain.**

• **How can the events in the lives of Joseph and his family serve as examples to prepare you for similar events?**

Allow some quiet time for the students to ask God for forgiveness for past actions of themselves or others, and to ask God for strength to walk closer to him in tough times that may come. Leave the "Spiritual Willpower" path available for teenagers to walk through during any free time for the rest of the day.

teaching session 3: practice makes perfect

Have students form pairs and say: **The next P that will help us in our quest is *practice*. When something difficult happens to us, it's easy to forget about God. Our minds are preoccupied with the situation, and we can't see how God can help us through it. In fact, our stress might even drive us to question God and his love for us. Practice helps us to pull God back into our lives when we need him the most.**

Turn off the lights and have audience members use flashlights as spotlights for situational skits. Choose one pair to go first, and have a volunteer stand by the light switch, ready to turn it off. Have each pair pull a "Practice Makes Perfect" slip of paper from the bag without reading it. Have the pair choose who will read the statement and who will react to it. Tell pairs that they will each role-play a situation in which two best friends are talking. One notices that something's the matter with the other person and asks what's wrong. After coaxing a little, the first person gets the second person to reveal a secret—

leader tip

You'll want to make sure the room is totally dark when the lights go off. Be sure to cover the windows with black plastic or blankets if it's still light out. If your retreat is outdoors, you may want to hold this activity around a campfire. Ask kids to sit silently and stare into the fire as the situation is revealed.

the situation that's noted on his or her paper slip.

As soon as the slip of paper is read, have your volunteer turn off the lights. Let everyone sit in darkness for about five seconds. Then ask audience members to ask questions of the actors one at a time, shining their flashlights as they ask. You might use questions such as the following to initiate the discussion:

- **How do you feel about what was just said?**

- **What will you say to your friend?**

- **Have you ever had this happen to you in real life? How did you react then?**

- **Would your faith be challenged if this situation really happened?**

- **What's the best reaction to this situation? the worst? How can your reaction help or hurt the other person?**

for younger teenagers

The situations for this activity are designed to be alarming; however, younger teenagers may have a more difficult time participating if the situations are too mature. You can tone down the situations by associating them with someone more distant—for example, changing "I have cancer" to "Your uncle has cancer." Or you can have small groups of younger teenagers discuss the difficult situations together. The bottom line is to make sure that younger teenagers can work on feeling comfortable about reacting to tough situations instead of acting immaturely.

Let everyone take turns in the role-play. When everyone has finished, ask pairs to read either Genesis 37; 39; 42; or 45. Then have pairs discuss these questions:

- **What was Joseph's tough situation?**

- **What was his knee-jerk reaction?**

- **How did Joseph rely on God?**

- **How can good things come from bad situations?**

- **Should you "practice" for bad things that might happen to you? Why or why not?**

After pairs have finished discussing, ask some of them to summarize their Bible stories for the rest of the students.

Say: **Joseph's life can help us to practice standing strong in tough situations. We all will face tough situations—but the toughest situation comes when we forget to rely on God when we need him the most.**

small-group discussion 2

Discuss these questions in your small group:

· Do you think people react differently in tough situations from the way they say they'll react? Why or why not?

· Is God in the equation when you face tough times? Why or why not?

· Have you ever blamed God for something bad that's happened to you? Explain.

· How can persisting, preparing, and practicing help you to rely on God when life is tough?

· Can you identify one way that you can prepare during the next week for tough times that might come in the future?

teaching session 4: prop it up with prayer, baby!

Say: **The last part of seeking God's face is key in helping you stand forever. It is something to rely on when you feel yourself weakening. Or it will strengthen you to the point that you don't even feel yourself weaken. Best of all, it gives you a way to strengthen someone else when you see their faith failing. The last P is to "Prop it up with prayer, baby!"**

Ask someone to read Psalm 105:1-4 aloud. Ask teenagers to name all the ways the writer mentions prayer or giving praise to God. Then ask: • **How can these aspects of prayer strengthen someone's faith?**

• **How can prayer help you make known among the nations what the Lord has done?**

• **How is standing strong easier with prayer for you? for others?**

Say: **You can never pray enough. Not only can you strengthen your own faith by opening up that communication with God, but you can prop others up with prayer when they need more strength.**

Hand out one resealable plastic bag with a handful of sand in it for each person. Keep a bag of sand for yourself. Place the large bottle in the center of the room.

Say: **Joseph was sent off into the desert in despair, made a slave, victimized, abandoned by family. And yet he became powerful and successful, and he saved his people from starvation because of his strength through God. This sand represents the barrenness of Joseph's situation. As we pray for ourselves and others,**

let's drop a grain of sand into the bottle to symbolize trusting God in the barren and difficult times we face in life.

Say a short prayer aloud as you drop a grain of sand into the large bottle. Say a second prayer and drop in a second grain of sand.

Say: **One or two grains of sand may seem hopeless, worthless. But God can count every grain of sand. And together, our prayers can build a foundation that can hold us up during tough times.**

Ask students to each hold a grain of sand, say silent prayers for strength in their own faith, then drop the grain of sand in the bottle. Then ask them to get another grain of sand and pray again, this time for someone else. Ask them to continue to pray this way for the next fifteen minutes. If they pray for a group of people, they can add a pinch of sand to the bottle. Let students know that you'll keep the bottle for youth meetings after the retreat, and students may keep their bags of sand; students will be able to continue to add sand to the bottle as they pray for themselves and others during tough times.

Close by asking each person to read Psalm 105:4 aloud, then to pray a sand-grain prayer for the person on the left to have strength to seek God's face always.

Student Quiet Time 1:
Imprisoned

Read Genesis 39:20-23. Imagine that you are Joseph. Take a few moments to write about what that would be like, based on this passage.

What are the things in your life that imprison you? What are the things that keep you distant from God?

How did Joseph's relationship with God help him survive imprisonment? How does *your* relationship with God survive tough times? Or does it?

Think about the item you chose last night to represent God's love for you. Tell God whether you feel "favored in his eyes." Tell God the ways that you see his love for you. Ask God to help you grow in that love.

STUDENT QUIET TIME 2: GOD ON MY MIND

Write down what your first thoughts of the day were when you woke up. Is God in them? How can you make him your first thought?

Write about how God fits in your life. How is God using your thoughts for his plans?

Read Genesis 45:5-7. How is God using the events in your life right now as a way to glorify his kingdom?

Spiritual Willpower

Instructions: Write these Scriptures and questions on the appropriate posters. Place the designated item and instructions regarding that item with each poster.

Family Problems

Item: house key

Read Genesis 45:12-14.

Instructions: Hold the house key in your hand and imagine yourself using it in your house at home.

Questions: Are you locking your front door to keep your family safe? Are you locking yourself in a room away from your family? Ask yourself whether the word *family* is more like "security" or "fear" to you, and think about why you feel that way.

Greed

Item: coins

Read Genesis 37:26-28.

Instructions: Count the money.

Questions: Have you ever turned away from your faith for money? How much money would you take to give up your relationship with God? What kind of wealth has God given you?

Jealousy

Item: mirror

Read Genesis 37:3-11.

Instructions: Hold up the mirror and look into it.

Questions: What do you look like when you are jealous? Does God see you that way?

Isolation

Item: blanket

Read Genesis 37:29-30.

Instructions: Cover yourself with the blanket as you answer the question below.

Questions: When you felt isolated, where was God? Did he abandon you? Did you abandon him?

Victimization

Item: none

Read Genesis 37:23-25.

Instructions: Close your eyes and think about the question below.

Question: How does knowing God is with you change whether you are a victim?

Disloyalty

Item: ring

Read Genesis 39:7-9.

Instructions: Place the ring on your finger.

Questions: Are you "married" to the people you love? In other words, are you committed to them? Are you loyal to them? Are they loyal to you? What do you want to say to the person who was disloyal to you? Or who you were disloyal to? What does God want to say to you about your loyalty to him?

Spiritual Willpower (continued)

Grief

Item: facial tissue

Read Genesis 37:34.

Instructions: none

Question: Do you blame God for your grief? Tell him why.

Misunderstanding

Item: puzzle piece

Read Genesis 42:36.

Instructions: Hold the puzzle piece in your hand.

Questions: Did you feel that everything was against you? What piece of the puzzle are you focused on? What part of the whole picture did you not see?

Lies

Items: box of crayons, paper

Read Genesis 37:20, 31-33.

Instructions: Open the box of crayons and draw your interpretation of what a lie is.

Questions: Do you know what a lie looks like? Did a lie hurt you? Was it harmless? Or did you lie—and why?

Resentment

Item: bottle

Read Genesis 42:8, 24.

Instructions: Open the bottle.

Questions: Do you let your feelings show? Or do you keep them bottled? How does God see your resentment?

Questioning God

Item: none

Read Genesis 42:28.

Instructions: none

Questions: What did God do to you? Why did you question him? Tell him about it.

Joy

Item: candle

Read Genesis 45:4-10.

Instructions: Choose one of the chairs, the stepladder, the table, or the rug to sit on, and focus on the candle from whatever station you chose.

Question: Where do you find light in the midst of darkness?

Humility

Item: none

Read Genesis 41:15-16.

Instructions: none

Question: How does humility glorify God?

Gifts

Item: wrapped gift box with gift tags

Read Genesis 40:6-8.

Instructions: Address the gift tag either to yourself or to someone who you've given your gifts to.

Questions: Joseph's gift was interpreting dreams. What is yours? How were you able to use it? Who benefited from your gift?

Practice Makes Perfect

Instructions: Cut apart these slips, fold them, and put them in a paper bag. (If you have more than twenty-two students, create more slips of paper with statements that could be really difficult for someone to deal with.)

- -

I'm dying.

- -

I'm dating your girlfriend (or boyfriend).

- -

I'm gay.

- -

Your father lost his job.

- -

I killed someone.

- -

My mother is an alcoholic.

- -

I don't want to live anymore.

- -

I have cancer.

- -

Someone stole your car.

- -

Your math teacher is flunking you.

- -

My father hits me.

- -

totally twisted priorities

master supply list

In addition to basic retreat supplies such as food, games, Bibles, pens, pencils, paper, and worship music, you'll also need the following supplies:

❑ a New International Version (NIV) Bible and one of the following: a New American Standard Bible (NASB), American Standard Version (ASV), or King James Version (KJV) Bible

❑ 1 piece of card stock for each student

❑ markers

❑ crayons

❑ 2 pieces of poster board

❑ 1 photocopy of "Small-Group Discussion 1" box (p. 143) for each small group

❑ 1 photocopy of "Student Quiet Time 1: Tombstone" (p. 148) for each student

❑ 1 photocopy of "Bid Sheet" handout (p. 150) for each student

❑ 26 paper plates

❑ roll of masking tape

❑ 2 identical jigsaw puzzles, both with at least as many pieces as the number of students

❑ puzzle glue (available at crafts stores)

❑ several games that involve timers (such as Boggle, Taboo, or Perfection)

❑ 1 photocopy of "Small-Group Discussion 2" box (p. 146) for each small group

❑ 1 photocopy of "Student Quiet Time 2: A Piece of the Puzzle" (p. 149) for each student

(continued on p. 142)

retreat focus: Students will reconsider their own life priorities as they study what the book of Ecclesiastes has to say about what's truly important in life.

retreat motto: Timing is everything—everything in its own time.

theme verse: "Now all has been heard; here is the conclusion of the matter: Fear God and keep his commandments, for this is the whole duty of man" (Ecclesiastes 12:13).

preparation

Before the retreat, gather all of the necessary supplies and make all of the photocopies recommended in the Master Supply List.

For Teaching Session 1, prepare the pieces of card stock by cutting them into the shape and approximate size of car license plates.

For Teaching Session 2, write each item from the "Bid Sheet" handout (p. 150) on a separate paper plate.

For Teaching Session 3, a few days before the retreat, prepare one of the jigsaw puzzles by putting it together and then applying several layers of puzzle glue (follow the directions on the glue) until the puzzle is completely stuck together.

For Teaching Session 4, you will need six different colored pieces of construction paper; each color will represent a different area of life. Use a marker to write one of the following life areas on each of the six colors of paper: family, school and activities, health, spiritual growth, friendship, and serving others.

Make sure students are divided into small groups (for more information on this, see p. 7), and take some time to study the book of Ecclesiastes on your own.

worship idea

For your theme song for the weekend, use "Once Again" from the two-CD set *I Could Sing of Your Love Forever*. For information on ordering student lyrics books, a song leader book, and the CDs, call Group at 1-800-447-1070.

suggested schedule

2-Night Retreat

Day	Time	Activity	Supplies
Friday	6:00-7:00 p.m.	Games	
	7:00-8:00 p.m.	Teaching Session 1: My Plate is Full	Bibles, various Bible translations, card stock, markers, pencils or pens, crayons, poster board, paper
	8:00-9:30 p.m.	Free Time	
	9:30-10:00 p.m.	Small Group Discussion 1	Photocopies of "Small-Group Discussion 1" box (p. 143)
	10:00-10:30 p.m.	Snacks	
	11:00 p.m.	Lights Out	
Saturday	7:30-8:00 a.m.	Student Quiet Time 1: Tombstone	Bibles, photocopies of "Student Quiet Time 1: Tombstone" (p. 148), pencils or pens
	8:00-9:00 a.m.	Breakfast	
	9:00-10:00 a.m.	Games	
	10:00-11:00 a.m.	Teaching Session 2: Going, Going, Gone!	Bibles, paper plates, photocopies of the "Bid Sheet" (p. 150), masking tape, paper, pencils or pens
	11:00 a.m.-noon	Lunch	
	noon-5:00 p.m.	Free Time or Group Activities	
	5:00-6:00 p.m.	Dinner	
	6:00-7:30 p.m.	Teaching Session 3: Time Out	Bibles, games, puzzle pieces, glued puzzle
	7:30-9:30 p.m.	Games or Group Activities	
	9:30-10:00 p.m.	Small-Group Discussion 2	Photocopies of "Small-Group Discussion 2" box (p. 146)
	10:00-10:30 p.m.	Snacks	
	11:00 p.m.	Lights Out	
Sunday	7:30-8:00 a.m.	Student Quiet Time 2: A Piece of the Puzzle	Bibles, photocopies of "Student Quiet Time 2: A Piece of the Puzzle" (p. 149), pencils or pens
	8:00-9:00 a.m.	Breakfast	
	9:00-10:00 a.m.	Teaching Session 4: The Whole Truth and Nothing But the Truth	Bibles, construction paper, stapler, crayons, markers
	10:00-11:00 a.m.	Worship Session: A Drop in the Bucket	Wash basin, water, plastic spoons
	11:00 a.m.-noon	Free Time or Group Activities	

Day	Time	Activity	Supplies
Friday	6:00-7:00 p.m.	Games	
	7:00-8:00 p.m.	Teaching Session 1: My Plate Is Full	Bibles, various Bible translations, card stock, markers, pencils or pens, crayons, poster board, paper
	8:00-9:30 p.m.	Free Time or Group Activities	
	9:30-10:00 p.m.	Small-Group Discussion 1	Photocopies of "Small-Group Discussion 1" box (p. 143)
	10:00-10:30 p.m.	Snacks	
	11:00 p.m.	Lights Out	
Saturday	7:30-8:00 a.m.	Student Quiet Time 1: Tombstone	Bibles, photocopies of "Student Quiet Time 1: Tombstone" (p. 148), pencils or pens
	8:00-9:00 a.m.	Breakfast	
	9:00-10:00 a.m.	Teaching Session 4: The Whole Truth and Nothing But the Truth	Bibles, construction paper, stapler, crayons, markers
	10:00-11:00 a.m.	Worship Session: A Drop in the Bucket	Wash basin, water, plastic spoons
	11:00 a.m.-noon	Free Time or Group Activities	

(continued from p. 140)

❏ sheets of multicolored construction paper. There should be at least 6 colors and enough paper so that each student can have 1 piece of each color of paper, plus 1 set for display.

❏ stapler and staples

❏ large wash basin

❏ 1 plastic spoon for each student

leader tip

For this "Totally Twisted" retreat, serve pretzel twists and Twizzlers candy as a snack. If you wake your group up with music, use songs like "The Twist" and "Twist and Shout."

teaching session 1: my plate is full

Ask: • **Does everyone know what "vanity plates" are?**

Explain to those who don't that they are license plates with catchy sayings on them such as "U R CUTE" or "K8S CAR" (Kate's car).

Say: **I want you to close your eyes and imagine you're rich. You have houses all over the world and a fleet of cars. There is one particular car that is your favorite. Imagine you are standing beside it now. The servants have finished waxing it. You hold in your hand the new vanity plate that will go on the back of your favorite car. Now open your eyes.**

Pass out the card stock "plates," and instruct the students to create their own vanity plates using the markers, crayons, and pencils. A design could include the person's name or some cute phrase that lets the world know "I am as cool as this car." When students complete their plates, have them hang them on the wall. Invite students to take turns explaining why they created the plates the way they did.

Ask: • **Why do you suppose they call these "vanity" plates?**

Give a volunteer an NASB, ASV, or KJV Bible and ask him or her to read Ecclesiastes 1:1-14 aloud.

Ask: • **When the writer says, "All is vanity," what do you think he means?**

• **What are some examples of vanity we see on TV, hear in songs, or see in magazines?**

Have another student read the same Scripture from the New International Version, then ask: • **What kinds of meaningless things do you see people investing time and energy into?**

• **We like stuff! We get our priorities twisted around. Can you think of something that you just "had to have" and worked to get it or whined to your parents for...only to have it sitting on a shelf a year later? What was it?**

• **Do you still need it?**

Have students form pairs and use paper and pencils to brainstorm lists of the top ten things that are most important in life. When pairs have completed their lists, they should read Ecclesiastes 1:16–2:16 and use the passage as an example to get them thinking about all the types of priorities, good and bad, that people pursue. Challenge each pair to come up with a second top ten list, this time containing the main activities, hobbies, or topics that use up a lot of their time, money, energy, and focus.

When they've finished, invite pairs to take turns shouting out the priorities from their lists of the things that are most important in life, and use their collective ideas to write a top ten list on a poster. Next ask them to shout out the top distractions—the list of things that consume people's energy, money, and time. Make another top ten list from these things, and hang both posters on the wall.

Say: **This weekend we're going to take some time to evaluate our priorities in life. There are tons of people we know and see on TV with really twisted priorities! There are lots of things, good and bad, that consume our energy, focus, time and money...but sometimes these things distract us from the things that should really be our top priorities.**

We're going to leave the vanity plates and these two lists up on the wall for the weekend. Look at them occasionally as we read and talk about what Ecclesiastes has to say.

small-group discussion 1

Discuss these questions with your small group:

· *Define the word* priority.

· *What are the top priorities for most of your friends at school?*

· *Do you agree that these things are meaningless? Why or why not?*

· *How can worldly values and priorities affect your relationship with God?*

teaching session 2: going, going, gone!

Before this session, tape the paper plates you prepared on the wall around the room in random order. Tape a blank piece of paper directly under each plate.

Ask: • **Has anybody ever sold or bought anything through an Internet auction?**

If someone has, ask him or her to explain the process. If no one is familiar with it, explain it this way: **In an online auction, you can find anything from used cars to movie props to antiques. If you want to buy something, you simply enter the amount you want to bid on that item and then every few days check back to see if you have been outbid by a buyer who is willing to pay more. At the end of a designated time period, if you are the highest bidder, you get to buy the product. We are going to have our own "online" auction today.**

Pass out photocopies of the "Bid Sheet" handout (p. 150) as well as pencils or pens.

Explain to students that they may spend a maximum of one thousand dollars. Have them first fill out the priority column, selecting the item they want the most and numbering it "1," then selecting their second highest priority and numbering it "2," and so on. Once they've done that, they should fill in the maximum bid column, keeping track of the most money they'd be willing to bid for each item, but making sure not to go over a total of one thousand dollars.

Say: **When I say "go," you can begin walking around the room placing bids on the items you want to buy. To bid, simply write your name and the amount you bid on the blank sheet of paper below the plate. If you are going to outbid someone else, just draw a line through the name and the amount bid, and write in your own name and bid amount. Make sure you check in on your previous bids to see if you need to make them higher. Only one person may bid on an item at a time, so form lines and take turns as you write down your bids. And remember, be careful when you bid—because you can't "take back" the amount you write down! For this reason you may want to begin by bidding smaller amounts. You have about fifteen minutes. Ready? Go.**

for younger teenagers

Middle school and junior high students may have a hard time prioritizing all of the available auction items. For younger teenagers, modify the list so that they only need to bid on a total of ten items. You may want to modify some of the items up for bid as well, such as replacing "a driver's license" with "an endless supply of pizza."

Call time after fifteen minutes, and gather up the bidding records below each plate, announcing each item winner and passing out the plates to the winners.

Have students form trios and discuss the following questions:

• **Which item was most important to you? Why?**

• **Which items held little or no value? Why?**

• **Sometimes it's easy to get our priorities twisted. How did you decide what was important and what wasn't?**

Have trios read Ecclesiastes 2:4-9, then ask: • **The writer of Ecclesiastes had all that he wanted. Was he a happy guy?**

• **Do you think those who "have it all" are happier because they do? Why or why not?**

• **What "twisted priorities" do you need to get out of your life?**

• **What forgotten priorities do you want to refocus on?**

Close by having trios pray for one another.

leader tip

Need game ideas? Check out the game book suggestions on page 7!

teaching session 3: time out

Before this session, set up several game stations (Boggle, Taboo, and so on) in various parts of the room.

Divide students into groups, one group for each game station you've set up. Tell students to begin playing the games, and after about five minutes yell "switch" and have groups rotate to the next game station and begin playing. Repeat this process of playing and switching games for twenty-five to thirty minutes.

When time is up, gather the groups together and ask:

• **Have you ever felt like this in real life? Like you're racing around, trying to beat the clock, trying to balance a lot of different activities? Explain.**

• **In some of these games, you had to rush to beat a timer—do you ever feel like you rush in real life? Explain.**

• **How do you think God wants you to balance all the demands on your time?**

Invite a student to read Ecclesiastes 3:1-8. Ask: • **Have you ever seen a little kid having to wait for mom or dad in a store? How do little kids wait?** (Have a volunteer show you an example.)

• **Are you ever like an impatient little kid when it comes to waiting for God's timing? Explain.**

• **How can relying on God's timing in our lives affect our priorities?**

Pass out the puzzle pieces. Say: **Let's assume this is your life or at least the part of your life you are familiar with. This is all you get to see.**

Get out the completed glued puzzle. Say: **This is what God sees—the "big picture."**

Ask: • **How can focusing on God's big picture for your life help you reconsider your priorities?**

Draw your students' attention to the top ten poster of the most important things in life from Teaching Session 1. Ask: • **How many of these things we listed should be big picture priorities for us?**

Have students hold their puzzle pieces tightly in their hands as you close in prayer.

small-group discussion 2

Discuss these questions with your small group:

· *What is your weekly schedule like? What sorts of things keep you busy?*

· *Do you ever struggle with trying to find a balance between focusing on big-picture stuff but getting caught up in a schedule full of busyness? Explain.*

· *What are the main big picture things you feel like you need to refocus on?*

· *Can you identify one action step you'll take in order to re-prioritize your schedule?*

teaching session 4:
the whole truth and nothing but the truth

Before this session, post the pieces of construction paper you prepared on the wall.

Begin by asking students to take ten minutes to glance through Ecclesiastes in their Bibles, trying to get a perspective of the overall tone of the book. When time is up, ask: • **In your own words, what is the main point of Ecclesiastes?**

• **What are your favorite verses in Ecclesiastes? Why?**

If students haven't already mentioned it, draw their attention to Ecclesiastes 12:13. Say: **Ecclesiastes is a book full of truths. It tells the truth about the meaningless-ness of self-centered pursuits. It is full of wise sayings and powerful statements. And it all boils down to one main point: The purpose of life is to honor and obey God. Only by focusing on God will we find contentment in life.**

Give each student six sheets of construction paper in different colors, as well as art supplies like crayons and markers. Tell them that, like the writer of Ecclesiastes, they're going to take some time to reflect on what is really important in life and then write down their conclusions. Point out the color chart you posted on the wall, and encourage each student to think of one "truth" to write concerning what is important in each of the following areas: family, school and activities, health, spiritual growth, friendship, and serving others. Explain that each colored piece of paper should correspond to the area of life indicated by that color on the color chart. (Students might write things such as

"The way I treat my friends matters to God—by showing them love I reflect God's character" or "Time spent having fun with my parents is more important than time spent staring at the TV.")

Challenge every student to also write one application statement for each category, beginning with the words "I will…"

Give students ample time to reflect and write their own "truth" books, stapling their pages together when they've finished writing. Wrap up the session by saying: **Getting our priorities "untwisted" will be a lifelong struggle. There will always be worries, activities, and material things competing for our time and attention, pulling our focus away from the truly important things in life. However, let's take to heart the message of Ecclesiastes—that our real purpose is to focus on God, not on things that are essentially meaningless.**

Ask students to join you in prayer, asking God for the strength to focus on the right priorities.

worship session: a drop in the bucket

If you are near an ocean or a lake, go to the beach. If not, fill a large wash basin with water, and have all the students gather around. Pass out a plastic spoon to each student.

Say: **Imagine we are on the beach. We are alone. I'm going to ask each of you to come up one at a time and take out a spoonful of water. Don't let it spill. Just take a spoonful and return to your place.**

While you say the following lines, point to one student to begin the process of taking spoonfuls of water. Say: **Let's imagine a million years have passed. Now another million years. Imagine that a million years have passed between each spoonful.**

After each student has taken a spoonful, say: **Imagine that we kept taking spoonfuls, one by one, until this body of water was emptied—dried out like a desert. Imagine a million years between each of those spoonfuls.**

Now prompt students to come forward one at a time and put their spoonful of water back in the basin. Say: **Again let's imagine that a million years have passed between each spoonful until the sea is full again.**

When the students have done that, say: **The amount of time it would take to empty the sea by spoonfuls in million-year intervals is absolutely incomprehensible—but it is only a blink of an eye to the God of eternity. Our lifetimes on earth, in the scope of eternity, are brief…short…over quickly. We must make the most of each day. We must use every day as a gift. We must get our priorities in order. All of the things that we put ahead of our relationship with God are vanities—they are meaningless.**

Invite all of the students to read Philippians 3:7-10 aloud in unison from their Bibles as your concluding prayer.

TOMBSTONE

Read Ecclesiastes 2:15-16.

The writer of Ecclesiastes wrote that all the things we build up in our lives don't amount to much when we are gone. Basically he's saying, "He who dies with the most toys…still dies." Take a moment and imagine your tombstone. Draw a picture of it. You don't have to put a date. Write a single word or phrase that you think will "sum it all up" for those who pass by your stone.

Sit quietly for a moment and think of all the things you have accomplished in your life so far (emotionally, physically, spiritually). How will these things benefit you down the road? Make a promise right now. (You can write it down if you want—no one will see this page.) Make a promise to yourself and to God that you will use one of those accomplishments for his glory. Write down one specific thing you can do to fulfill that promise in the next week, the next year, or the next ten years.

Student Quiet Time 2:

A Piece of the Puzzle

(Instructions: Get your puzzle piece from Teaching Session 3 and use it for this Quiet Time.)

Think of your puzzle piece as just one piece of your life—one stage. Trace your puzzle piece here. (If you can't find it right now, draw one.)

Now think of all the other stages of your life—your past…your future. They make up the big picture of your life. What values are reflected in the picture? What is most important to you? What have you done with your life? What will you do? What will you focus on?

Read Ecclesiastes 3:14.

Now *that's* the real big picture. God is eternal. God's works are eternal.

God wants to use you to do eternal things—to make an eternal difference. Prayer, love, kindness, selflessness…all of these things make an eternal difference.

Write out a prayer to the God of eternity—the God who holds your puzzle piece in his hands.

Bid Sheet

Instructions: You have a maximum of $1,000 to spend bidding for the items on this list. First, read through the list and rank the items according to how important they are to you—do this in the Priority column. If you aren't interested in some of them, just give them a "zero" priority. Next figure out the maximum amount of money you'd be willing to spend on your top priority items, and put that in the Maximum Bid column—but remember, you can't spend more than a *total* of $1,000!

Item	Priority	Maximum Bid	Final Payment
Straight A's on your next report card			
Life without zits			
A supermodel's body			
A brand-new SUV			
A mansion by the sea			
Perfect dance moves			
A maid to clean your room for one year			
A magic homework wand			
A family that never argues			
The ability to play guitar			
Teeth that don't need braces			
A college scholarship to anywhere			
A photographic memory			
A driver's license			
A closet full of brand-new clothes			
A car that will get me to school			
A house with a pool			
Total Bible recall			
To change one thing about me physically			
To move to another state			
A fantastic girlfriend			
A fantastic boyfriend			
Thirty extra minutes of sleep every Sunday			
A weekend vacation anywhere in the world with my best friend			
The ability to fly			
For my parents to be happy			

Group Publishing, Inc.
Attention: Product Development
P.O. Box 481
Loveland, CO 80539
Fax: (970) 679-4370

Evaluation for
Go Deeper Retreats

Please help Group Publishing, Inc. continue to provide innovative and useful resources for ministry. Please take a moment to fill out this evaluation and mail or fax it to us. Thanks!

● ● ●

1. As a whole, this book has been (circle one)

not very helpful   very helpful

1   2   3   4   5   6   7   8   9   10

2. The best things about this book:

3. Ways this book could be improved:

4. Things I will change because of this book:

5. Other books I'd like to see Group publish in the future:

6. Would you be interested in field-testing future Group products and giving us
   your feedback? If so, please fill in the information below:

Name _____

Church Name _____

Denomination _____ Church Size _____

Church Address _____

City _____ State _____ ZIP _____

Church Phone _____

E-mail _____

Grab Students' Hearts and Go Deeper!

Ultimate Skits: 20 Parables for Driving Home Your Point

Bryan Belknap

Jesus used parables to connect spiritual truth with people's lives. Do the same with these 20 attention-grabbing, "non-cheesy", funny modern parables for students. These 5-minute skits include powerful discussion questions on topics that interest students: media influence, hypocrisy, God's love, violence and more!

ISBN 0-7644-2354-1 $16.99

Faith Metaphors: 50 Interactive Object Lessons for Youth Ministry

Remember the fish and loaves? The unforgettable point Jesus made? Make powerful points like that in every lesson or study! 50 fresh, easy object lessons to involve students in topics like: Following God, Dating, God's Love, and more. Add to your lessons or use as lessons!

ISBN 0-7644-2301-0 $15.99

JumpStarters: 100 Games to Spark Discussions

These 100 "fun-with-a-purpose" games are sure to ignite conversation among your teenagers on 43 relevant topics, such as worship, peer pressure, dating, and God's love. Includes strategic questions to guide discussion and a Scriptural and topical index!

ISBN 0-7644-2219-7 $15.99

Diving Deep: Experiencing Jesus Through Spiritual Disciplines

Amy Simpson

Dive deep into traditional spiritual disciplines like worship, solitude, prayer, fasting, and others. This flexible, interactive course contains 13 lessons, a complete retreat plan and 6 student journals. Perfect for students at any spiritual level, in any ministry setting.

ISBN 0-7644-2341-X $49.99

Diving Deep Student Journal

ISBN 0-7644-2388-6 $6.99

Prayer in Motion: Leading Students in Life-Changing Prayer

Help your students develop dynamic prayer lives with this multimedia prayer adventure. This Kit features an easy-to-use, four session Leader Guide that culminates in a "concert of prayer" event; six Student Prayer Journals; a compelling prayer montage video, and a worship CD. Equip your students to pray with power, purpose and persistence.

ISBN 0-7644-2387-8 $79.99

Prayer in Motion - Prayer Journal

ISBN 0-7644-2401-7 $6.99

High-Impact Youth Ministry Resources

All-Star Games From All-Star Youth Leaders

The ultimate game book—from the biggest names in youth ministry! All-time, no-fail favorites from Wayne Rice, Rich Mullins, Tiger McLuen, Darrell Pearson, Bart Campolo, Steve Fitzhugh, and others! A mix of icebreakers, mixers, and off-the-wall games.

ISBN 0-7644-2020-8 **$15.99**

The Gigantic Book of Games for Youth Ministry, Volumes 1 & 2

Never be caught flat-footed at game time again! Here are a whopping 300 games gathered from veteran youth workers! You get team-building games, Bible-learning games and energy-burning games. You'll always find the right game for any meeting…any lesson…any time!

Volume 1 **ISBN 0-7644-2113-1** **$21.99**
Volume 2 **ISBN 0-7644-2089-5** **$21.99**

The Youth Bible

Your teenagers will read *The Youth Bible*. The clear, understandable text really speaks to kids. And so do 400 compelling, real-life devotions on topics your kids care about. Get your kids to read the Bible…order today!

Hardcover **ISBN 0-7180-0118-4** **$24.99**
Softcover **ISBN 0-7180-0117-6** **$19.99**

Experiencing the Trinity: The 3-in-1 Gift Set

Encounter God in Three Persons: Father, Son, Holy Spirit

This 3-book devotional set is the perfect gift for yourself or someone you care about. You'll realize that God is close to you every minute of every hour of every day. A total of 90 activities that will be unforgettable "God moments" in your life. Includes the best-selling devotional/journals: *God Is Near, Christ In Me,* and *The Spirit Moves.*

ISBN 0-7644-2422-X **$24.99**

Doing Life With God: Real Stories Written by High School Students

Bo Boshers with Kim Anderson

Designed to encourage and help youth through the common struggles they face with 30 devotions written by Christian students who speak from experience. Great as an individual study of for groups to study together.

ISBN 0-7644-2227-8 **$7.99**

Doing Life With God 2: Real Stories Written by Students

Bo Boshers with Kim Anderson

30 devotions written by Christian students who've "been there" and gone through what your teenagers and their friends face. Each devotion has small group questions and a personal journal exercise! Encourage and inspire your teenagers to "do life" with God every day!

ISBN 0-7644-2228-6 **$7.99**

Bo Boshers is the Executive Director of Student Ministries in the Willow Creek Association. A worldwide speaker and best-selling author with over 20 years of ministry experience, Bo teamed up with high school students from around the world to create these compelling compilations of real-life stories.

Maximize Your Youth Ministry

Finding the Faith Devotions for Youth Ministry

Creative, heart-gripping interactions give students fresh insights into Bible-based Christian beliefs. Easy to prepare and lead, these 40 bite-size devotions will trigger "no boredom" discussions on topics like the Church, God's love, sin and forgiveness, salvation, and others! Great for any area of youth ministry!

ISBN 0-7644-2200-6 $15.99

The Top 20 Messages for Youth Ministry

Jim Kochenburger

20 complete, cutting-edge message outlines! Need major sizzle, a sprinkling of spice or the whole enchilada (whole messages)? You'll find what you need in *The Top 20 Messages for Youth Ministry*! Features 20 topical outlines with Bible-based points; over 20 great stories and illustrations; more than 20 great movie clip illustration ideas; over 50 quick and easy ideas for involving group members in your message; and, a boatload of extra ideas! Take your speaking to the next level!

ISBN 0-7644-2258-8 $15.99

I Could Sing of Your Love Forever Lyrics Book

This stunning collection includes 25 of the top worship songs of our time! You get the complete lyrics for songs like *Open the Eyes of My Heart, Shout to the Lord, The Happy Song, What A Friend I've Found*, and the title song. Songs from the leading worship artists of our day, including Matt Redman, Martin Smith, Delirious?, Sonic Flood, and The Burn Service.

Student Lyrics Book   Item #3067XA $3.99

Group's BlockBuster Movie Illustrations: Over 160 Clips for Your Ministry!

Bryan Belknap

Press "PLAY" for your students' attention! Use clips from popular movies to illustrate what the Bible says about issues teenagers face. Each clip reference includes "where-you-live" discussion questions to get youth talking! Scripture and theme indexes included. Keep ministry relevant!

ISBN 0-7644-2256-1 $15.99

The Prayer Path: A Christ-Centered Labyrinth Experience
In partnership with Proost Productions

With *The Prayer Path*, churches will create their own multi-media labyrinth, a unique guided prayer and devotional adventure. Participants will "journey" through the labyrinth over the span of about an hour guided by a CD that soars with provocative, devotional narration set against a worshipful music backdrop. This can comes packed with sight-and-sound tools you'll need for offering an exceptional encounter with God at your next church special event, retreat, camp, or an innovative, spiritually compelling community outreach: a Leader guide, 10 participant devotional guides, 6 accompanying CD audio guides, two videos all in a can.

ISBN 0-7644-1303-1 $79.99

1 gallon can, Leader Guide (64 pages), 10 Participant Guides (32 pages), 6 CDs and 2 videos

Additional CDs

6 CD set	UPC 646847-11532-5	**$59.99**
Single CD	UPC 646847-11542-4	**$15.99**

Additional Participant Guides

10 pack	ISBN 0-7644-1310-4	**$4.99**